CRUISERS
IN CAMERA

HMS *Glasgow* (1936); see also p. 101. Seen here on 14 June 1953, she is wearing the flag of the CinC Mediterranean, Admiral Lord Mountbatten, while at Spithead for the Coronation Review of the Fleet. After a refit at Chatham in 1951, during which the bridge was modified and all 20 mm guns removed, she became flagship of the CinC Mediterranean. Her close-range armament now comprises six quad pom-poms and eight single 'Boffins' – 40 mm Bofors guns on twin 20 mm power mountings. Two of the latter are unusually sited at the aft corners of B gun deck. Her sensors include a YE-60 aircraft homing beacon on a mast to starboard of the second funnel, and radar Types 284 on the DCT, with the more modern Type 277Q on the lattice tower behind it, Type 285 on the three HACS and Type 281B plus its associated IFF at the head of the mainmast. At the end of 1943 the *Glasgow*, together with the old cruiser *Enterprise* (see p. 84), had fought a successful action against a force of German flotilla craft. Damaged by shore batteries during D Day operations in June 1944, she underwent repairs and a refit which included the removal of X turret. At the same time her anti-aircraft armament and radar outfit were enhanced. The *Glasgow* was sold for scrap in 1958. (*Ian Allan/Science Museum/Science & Society S2516*)

CRUISERS
IN CAMERA

ROGER HAYWARD

SUTTON PUBLISHING LIMITED

First published in 2000 by
Sutton Publishing Limited · Phoenix Mill
Thrupp · Stroud · Gloucestershire · GL5 2BU

British Library Cataloguing in Publication Data
A catalogue record for this book is available from the British Library

ISBN 0 7509 2350 4

Typeset in 11/15pt Baskerville MT
Typesetting and origination by
Sutton Publishing Limited
Printed in Great Britain by
Butler & Tanner, Frome, Somerset

CONTENTS

ACKNOWLEDGEMENTS

First, I wish to offer my grateful thanks to the private individuals and to the staff of the navies, museums, agencies and other collections worldwide who have made available photographs for this book. It is only through their kind and patient co-operation that so many new or rarely-seen images have been obtained. Individual acknowledgements of ownership are placed under each illustration. Special thanks are offered to the Fleet Air Arm Museum, the National Maritime Museum, the Plymouth Naval Base Museum, the Portsmouth Royal Dockyard Historical Trust and the Science Museum for allowing me unrestricted access to their collections. Prints of photographs may be purchased directly from most public and commercial agencies and collections.

In the United Kingdom we are fortunate in having an unrivalled archive of British warship photographs at the sources credited, and elsewhere. We should be grateful for the foresight of those who have preserved this material. The collections overseas are often full of pleasant surprises for the researcher.

My sincere thanks go also to my publisher for not complaining when I missed deadlines.

Finally, I should like to express my grateful thanks to my wife for her patience during the long gestation period of this book, and to apologize to my friends for neglecting them.

Roger Hayward
January 2000

INTRODUCTION

This book is not a complete history of British cruisers: such a study has yet to be produced. Rather, it is a selective and affectionate glance, springing from a love of cruisers and their aesthetics. Beauty is, of course, in the eye of the beholder, and individuals will have their own tastes. However, it was easier for cruisers to be endowed with good looks than for most other types of warship, for they tended to have length without huge bulk. Many will agree that some, such as the Warriors of the 1900s and the Counties of the 1920s, had a massive grandeur; some, such as the Cambrian and Hawkins classes, displayed a pleasing elegance; while of the others the Amphions of the 1930s were gifted with an unmatched balanced purity of line which was surely the result of genius in the design office. There were, of course, less pleasing classes. Many Victorian ships had very thin stove-pipe funnels, while a large gap between bridge and fore funnel would upset the balance of a design. Boxy aircraft hangars marred many later ships. However, being quite properly preoccupied with greater priorities, designers did not set out to produce appealing ships. That they often did so was a bonus.

Although appealing lines do not them-selves make for an efficient design, British cruisers generally performed well during the two world wars. Losses were heavy because they were worked hard, but they generally proved tough ships. They were susceptible to underwater damage, but then so were contemporary capital ships. Their greatest strength was dependability. However, a lack of speed could allow a flying enemy, Austrian or German, to escape in the First World War, while their greatest weakness in the Second World War was a lack of effective light anti-aircraft guns and of sufficient ammunition to feed them.

In general, the ships were handled boldly and well, but in the First World War the largest cruisers suffered badly. As well as the Battle of Jutland, where light cruisers acquitted themselves well but cruisers were misemployed, there was in 1914 the dis-tasteful affair of a British cruiser squadron refusing battle. In contrast the lighter ships won great acclaim. In the Second World War an underestimation of air power and a lack of defence against it caused grievous damage off Norway, Crete and Ceylon. On the other hand aggressive handling against the odds brought excellent results in the South Atlantic, the Arctic and the Mediterranean.

In the heyday of sail there was no such type of vessel as the cruiser. Any warship, from a Third Rate (74 gun) ship of the line to a sloop or even smaller, could be sent on a cruising commission. Although the sailing frigate is often regarded as the forerunner of the modern cruiser, that actually evolved into the single-gun-deck iron battleship of the Warrior type. 'Cruiser' was a rôle, not a ship type. That rôle might encompass such functions as trade protection and the interdiction of an enemy's trade, scouting and despatch work, training cruises, Showing the Flag around the Empire and in foreign ports, and acting as a ship of force, in lieu of a capital ship, on distant stations. The range of possible duties was and remained large and the range in size of the ships intended to fulfil these duties was equally broad. In the twentieth century it also encompassed the escorting of larger warships and shore bombardment. After the Second World War there was little except the latter that other smaller and newer types could not do better than the surviving cruisers.

Between the revolutionary Warrior class battleships of 1860 and the emergence of the classic pre-Dreadnought a quarter of a century later, battleship development was punctuated by a series of false steps and blind alleys. In contrast, the lineage of the cruiser from the first iron-hulled ships onwards was a relatively smooth and logical progression. There were some unsuccessful developments: the torpedo cruiser, which was neither a cruiser nor a success; and the final classes of armoured cruiser, which were unnecessarily capable for cruiser work and too weak for anything else (their greatest sin was that they led to the battlecruiser). Wooden construction persisted in smaller cruisers, while sailing rig was retained later than in battleships because coaling stations were scarce in some parts of the world. Later, coal *v.* oil brought similar arguments as sail *v.* steam.

The freak Austro/Italian naval action at Lissa in 1866 led most of the world's major warships, including cruisers, to be designed with a ram, or, later, cutaway ram, bow for some fifty years. The former made for excessive wetness over the forecastle deck. The feature could be taken to extremes, culminating in the Arrogant class, broad-beamed 2nd class protected cruisers with specially strengthened hulls forward, being termed 'fleet rams'.

In 1890 all the many old categories of cruisers, including cruising vessels and screw corvettes, which were not 'armoured' and therefore 1st class, were recategorized as 'protected cruisers', according to the thickness of their protective deck. At a stroke classes of 1st, 2nd and 3rd class protected cruisers were created. Broadly speaking, these had a protective armoured deck of 4 in or more, over 2 in and 2 in or less respectively, at about waterline level and often over the whole length of the ship. All coal-burning ships derived additional protection from the coal in their bunkers, positioned between the ship's vitals and the sides of the hull. Because of the great weight of compound armour, most Victorian cruisers lacked armoured sides and relied instead on a protective deck over their vitals, up to 6 in thick in a few of the largest. The great disadvantage of this system was that, despite the protection afforded by the coal bunkers, shells would enter and explode inside the hull. The thick deck would hopefully keep splinters away from boilers, engines and magazines, but the upper hull would be wrecked and heavy casualties suffered. Guns and their crews had their own protection. However, unnecessary casualties occurred, as some gun shields did not extend down to deck level.

A breakthrough came with the development of hard-faced steel armour, which initially had the same resistant properties as compound armour some 108 per cent thicker. This allowed cruisers to carry a deep armour belt of adequate resistance, without the need to compromise on engine power and fuel capacity. The first cruisers to be given a steel armour belt were the armoured cruisers of the Cressy class (1899), whose 6 in belts were the equivalent of over 12 in of the old compound armour. A further twenty-nine ships of six more classes, and of up to almost 15,000 tons, followed. Sixteen of these were overt counters to large foreign commerce raiders. The other nineteen were armed with 9.2 in guns and were regarded as a potential fast light wing of the battle fleet: ships which would smother damaged enemy battleships with rapid fire from their medium-calibre guns at comparatively close range. However, they too had a trade-protection rôle. By 1914 battle ranges had increased enormously, and the concept was rendered obsolete. Unfortunately, that fact had not been heeded, and three of the largest armoured cruisers were lost to the gunfire of German capital ships at the Battle of Jutland.

Side armour was not introduced into smaller cruisers until the Chatham class of 1911. Because this side armour was thin and of small area, the ships were described as 'belted', rather than 'armoured'. Armour belts were designed to keep out enemy shells: they offered scant protection from underwater damage by mines and torpedoes. These frequently proved fatal to even the largest and most modern capital ships and, being smaller and less able to absorb damage, cruisers often suffered badly.

For all duties except for hunting the most powerful commerce-raiders it was the 2nd class cruiser, the backbone of the Victorian cruiser force, which most closely met the Royal Navy's needs. However, of the seventy-three cruisers begun after the first of the Arrogants in June 1895 until the first of the Bristols of February 1909, only five were of this useful type. Although the 2nd class vessels of the Town classes were relatively successful, it was the weaker new scout cruisers that established the line of development that led to the Arethusa class, which entered service at the outbreak of war. This line continued to the Emeralds, which did not complete until 1926.

The first battlecruisers were contemporaneous with the last armoured cruisers, and large cruisers fell out of favour for a decade, the few new schemes drawn up being still-born. The next large big-gunned ships, the Hawkins class, were radically different, being powerful ships of high speed and exceptional endurance, but with light cruiser protection, albeit on a much-extended scale. Not only was there side protection up to forecastle deck level, but also the class introduced box protection, a feature not usually listed among ships' specifications, whereby magazines and other internal vitals could be given all-round local protection with little weight penalty. The first was laid down in 1915 and the last was still at sea in 1947. Another nine years passed before the first of the next (and what, with the two Yorks, turned out to be last) group of large big-gunned ships, the County classes, appeared. These were the first cruisers begun after the First World War.

The building of light cruisers began again in 1930, when HMS *Leander* was laid down. There followed into service a fairly logical succession of thirty-two medium to large ships, from the five Leanders to the Minotaur/Tiger class. Three more hulls of the latter type, suspended because they were too late for the Second World War, were begun again after the Korean War and completed to a radical new design with a few automatic guns. These three were unsuccessful, unloved and too expensive to run. After little service, two were converted to command/helicopter ships. To meet the demand for quantity, even at the expense of quality, small cruisers also continued to be laid down between 1933 and 1940. The first four were three-turret versions of the Amphions (modified Leanders), the other sixteen were dual-purpose vessels which introduced a new 5.25 in gun which had a good anti-aircraft performance.

Anti-aircraft weapons had been fitted to cruisers since early in the First World War. The exaggerated fear of high-level bombing was countered by the 4 in HA/LA gun. An increasing awareness of the potency of the torpedo-bomber led to the development of the 40 mm 2 pdr pom-pom and, for last-ditch defence, the quadruple 0.5 in heavy machine-gun firing solid shot. The pom-pom, on which much faith was pinned, was installed in single, octuple and later, starting with the new Towns, quadruple mountings. The need for the multiple pom-pom was identified in 1921, but twenty years later, in the darkest days of the Second World War, there were still not enough for the fleet's needs. Unfortunately, although it produced an impressive volume of fire, the pom-pom was relatively ineffective against the Second World War aircraft, as it had a low muzzle velocity (the 0.5 in machine-gun was even less effective). Early in the war a few ships were unlucky enough to be fitted with heavy twenty-barrelled launchers for Unrotated Projectiles, a useless device for dangling parachute-suspended bombs into the path of enemy aircraft. That was the theory, but it did not work. Reliance came to be placed on the 20 mm Oerlikon and, later, the 40 mm Bofors guns. But these foreign weapons were in short supply and arrived too late to save many grievous losses.

Against submarines, the defence offered by high speed could not be used in situations such as convoy escort and shore bombardment, and reliance had to be placed on escort vessels. Moored mines were recognized as a major threat in Victorian times, against which paravanes were only partially successful, but degaussing coils offered some protection against Second World War magnetic ground mines.

The older cruisers of the First World War were powered by huge triple-expansion reciprocating engines, which, with so many heavy moving parts, could be unreliable and difficult to maintain, although far better than the technology they replaced. Introduced in the 1880s the largest had four cylinders and developed up to 30,000 indicated horsepower, but the *Amethyst* of 1903 employed experimental steam turbine machinery. The advantages were enormous and from 1908 onwards turbines became standard. Coal-firing gradually gave way to oil, via oil-sprayed coal, geared turbines were introduced, and lighter small-tube boilers of increased working pressure gradually, too gradually, came into use. The speed of major surface fighting ships peaked in late-First World War designs.

During the latter part of the First World War a number of fast light cruisers carried fighters on fixed short take-off ramps for use against snooping Zeppelins. The next development was the revolving aircraft flying-off platform, shortly followed by the vastly superior revolving or, later, fixed catapult for launching reconnaissance seaplanes. These could land alongside and be recovered by crane. The introduction of radar at the end of the 1930s led to the gradual disappearance of catapult aircraft, for it could detect not only ships but also aircraft, and it was but a short step to becoming an invaluable aid to gunnery and navigation.

The periods of tension leading to both world wars found the Royal Navy with numerous small obsolete cruisers which, through shortage of funds and shipyard facilities, could not be replaced. New life was breathed into some by converting them to hitherto-unforeseen duties. The expending of a few as blockships or break-waters was no loss to the navy.

A shortage of first quality ships of all types, especially cruisers, was a problem that continually hampered the Royal Navy. As the need for stronger armament, greater protection, higher speed and longer endurance increased over the decades, so in parallel did relative costs. This invariably meant that insufficient new cruisers were built and too few sound ships were modernized. The British Empire was so far flung that it was impossible to defend it all, together with its connecting trade routes, simultaneously. This did not matter too much for most of the nineteenth century, when there were no serious challenges. However, actual or potential threats from France, Russia and then Germany eventually placed demands on the navy which it

could not meet. A consensus between HM Treasury, the Foreign and the Colonial Offices on what policies should be pursued, what possessions could be defended and therefore retained, and how defending them adequately against simultaneous aggression in several theatres should be financed, was never reached – or perhaps not even considered. Ship design was compromised by a refusal to spend money on building work to enlarge dry docks, just as, later, heavy bomber design was compromised by a reluctance to spend a little money on widening aircraft hangars. The Treasury would never fund the provision of sufficient first-class material, whether it be ships, aircraft or rifles, it being cheaper to send inadequately equipped men to their deaths.

The passage of time has left us with few reminders of this important and once-numerous family of ships. There is, of course, the *Belfast*, but it is a pity that the incomparably more interesting and representative HMS *Sheffield* was not retained instead. We are fortunate that one even older ship, HMS *Caroline*, remains as an as-yet uncut jewel in the United Kingdom's maritime crown. This First World War veteran, the last survivor of the Battle of Jutland, is currently still in the safe hands of the Royal Navy. However, the time will eventually come for her disposal, and when that happens it would be a national tragedy if she was not to be placed in the hands of fully funded restorers of the quality who gave the 1860 battleship HMS *Warrior* back to the nation, rather than be passed to mere preservationists.

In all but one case the sequence followed in the pictorial sections of this work places the classes in order of the date on which the first ship of a class or subclass was laid down. In this way it is hoped that the progression of design trends may be more apparent. To comply with tradition, the date shown against each ship's name is the year in which it was launched.

As this brief study of British and Australian-built cruisers will concentrate on those classes which served in or were intended to serve in the two world wars, only the major milestones leading to the late-Victorian ships are considered. Every class is illustrated, although of course not every ship. Apart from the first four and the last, all the plates illustrate ships which served during or were built to serve in the two world wars. In a number of cases, more than one image of a particular ship has been included in order to show the effect of progressive refits and alterations. There are images from the building slip to the breaker's yard. A number of cruisers built for the Royal Navy served with other forces, including those of the Commonwealth. Many of these, together with those ships built specifically for the Royal Australian Navy, will be found in Chapter 6. Where these are of rarity value, some images of imperfect quality have been included throughout.

Although a degree of balance has been sought, particular emphasis has been given to the significant Hawkins and County classes, respectively the models for and result of the cruiser limits in the important 1922 Washington Naval Treaty. Wartime operations are briefly touched on only.

All dimensions, place-names, etc., are those of the cruiser era. One anomaly is that light guns were indiscriminately described by imperial or metric calibres or by weight of shot: 12 pounder (pdr) was 3 in, 6 pdr was 57 mm, 3 pdr was 47 mm and 2 pdr was 40 mm. As both the Vickers and Bofors AA cannon were 40 mm 2 pdrs, they are generally referred to as pom-poms and Bofors respectively. One knot is one nautical mile of 6,080 ft per hour. One ton is 2,240 lbs.

1 IN THE BEGINNING

With the introduction of the iron-built Warrior class battleships in 1860, a new age in naval shipbuilding dawned: one no less significant than the appearance some forty-five years later of HMS *Dreadnought*. The iron battleship left the wooden cruising ship behind, literally, as wooden construction limited the size and therefore the engine power of any vessel. Wooden cruisers were slower than the latest capital ships for which they might be required to scout, and were slower than many ocean liners which they might wish to attack or protect. The move to iron construction for cruising warships was inevitable and HMS *Inconstant* (1868) and her near-sister-ship *Shah* were the first. They were quite similar in concept and layout to the Warrior class battleships, except that they were unarmoured – although, as in all coal-burners, their bunkers offered limited protection and buoyancy. These two large and successful ships were inspired by the performance of fast commerce raiders during the American Civil War. The US Navy's Wampanoag class of commerce-raiding cruisers was viewed with alarm by the Admiralty, particularly as the United States was then a potential enemy, and these ships therefore posed a serious threat to British shipping. The 6,000 ton *Inconstant* and *Shah* were ordered in response. Better ships in every way, they were fast in service, as opposed to on paper, making over 16 knots under steam and a good 13 knots under sail, and carried a heavy armament.

Slow cruisers continued to be built, including more wooden ships: the last being launched in 1874. However, the value of these was strictly limited and gradual progress was made in several directions. The first armoured cruisers appeared in 1875. In these, the ship's vitals, but not the gun battery, were protected by both an armoured deck and a belt of thick compound armour. This was excessively heavy and only a shallow belt could be provided. Although powerfully armed, these ships were too slow for true cruiser work and instead acted as 2nd class capital ships on distant stations.

The next milestone came in the form of the very fast small cruisers *Iris* and *Mercury* of 1877. The fastest ships in the world at the time, this pair were the Royal Navy's first steel warships and can be regarded as the prototypes of all subsequent cruisers. Although twice as expensive, early steel was some 30 per cent stronger than wrought iron, allowing weight to be diverted towards engines, fuel or armament, or a proportion of each. The savings available had gone into the provision of 7,500 ihp compound engines, giving a speed of some 18.5 knots, a vital margin of speed over the contemporary battle fleet. Compared to earlier

ROYAL NAVY

Inconstant Group 2nd Class Unprotected Cruisers – three ships, first of group laid down in November 1866. Legend displacement 5,780 tons (*Inconstant*); length and beam 337 ft 4 in (pp) × 50 ft 3 in; power 7,360 ihp for 16 kts; principal armament: ten 9 in and six 7 in guns, two carriages for 16 in torpedoes.

HMS *Inconstant* (1868). The first British iron-hulled cruiser, the *Inconstant* was a remarkably fast ship for her time, achieving 16.5 kts in shallow water during steaming trials on 16 July 1869, and capable of 13.5 kts under sail. Her heavy armament of rifled muzzle-loading guns enabled her to fight at long range, where her unarmoured hull would be less vulnerable. For protection, her hull was subdivided up to the main deck by ten watertight bulkheads. The one weakness of these ships was cost, and the design was not repeated. The *Inconstant* remained active until 1897. Later, in 1920, she was attached to the old 'wooden wall' HMS *Defiance*, by then a training hulk, (see also next plate) and was scrapped as late as 1956. (*Plymouth Naval Base Museum*)

classes their sailing rig was light, although it remained an important asset when the ships were conceived.

In the late 1870s improvements in the power and range of cruiser guns led to abandonment of the unarmoured cruiser and the introduction of the protected cruisers described in the introduction. The classes of smaller cruisers developed through such types as the 'masted' Leanders of 1882 (improved successors of the Mercurys) to the tiny (1,770 ton) Archer class.

A shortage of coaling facilities around the world initially caused the retention of sail in many cruisers, but the situation gradually improved to the extent that 'mastless' ships could be introduced. The Imperieuse class armoured cruisers, which

HMS *Defiance*, the Torpedo School at Plymouth. Three old cruisers, the Diadem class *Andromeda* (1897), the *Inconstant* and the *Vulcan* (a 6,629 ton torpedo boat-carrying cruiser of 1889), formed the *Defiance* Torpedo School in early 1931. They are seen moored in the Hamoaze off Cove Head, with a Dido class cruiser stern-on to the *Andromeda*, in 1950. All retain the old black, white and buff Victorian livery of the previous century. The Torpedo School was closed in 1954 and, sadly, the old ships were sold for scrap, the *Vulcan* in 1955 and the *Andromeda* in 1956. (*Royal Navy*)

introduced the 9.2 in gun in 1883, had their sailing rig removed, which greatly improved them. The next class was an important milestone, being the first cruisers to be designed with no sailing rig at all, full trust being placed in the universal availability of coal. These were the four Mersey class protected cruisers of 1885. Useful ships, the last survived in South Africa until 1947 (see Chapter 6). They were followed by the seven Orlando class ships of 1886, the first armoured cruisers designed to bear no canvas. Although so overweight that their shallow armour belt was submerged, they were nevertheless reasonably sound vessels, with all their major guns mounted at the same height. Their balanced two-funnel two-mast profile set the trend for many future classes.

The torpedo cruiser was devised to take the efficient new-pattern torpedo to sea in pre-submarine days. For success it needed high speed, adequate endurance and good seakeeping, but the sixteen ships of this type successfully managed to avoid all these virtues. With their small size and short endurance they were not true cruisers. Another way of getting the torpedo to sea was to carry small steam torpedo boats to the action on a much larger vessel. The more promising of two experiments was the 20 knot *Vulcan*, a large and fully seaworthy vessel which was similar to the roughly contemporary Edgar class cruisers, except that she lacked heavy guns. Instead, she carried six 2nd class torpedo boats. This experiment was not repeated, presumably because of the difficulty of launching and recovering the flimsy craft close to an enemy.

Iris Class 2nd Class Unprotected Cruisers – two ships, first of class laid down in November 1875. Legend displacement 3,730 tons; length and beam 315 ft (333ft *Iris*) overall × 56 ft; power 6,000 ihp for 17 kts; principal armament: ten 64 pdr guns, four 16 in torpedo carriages.

HMS *Mercury* (1878). Seen in March 1890, prior to departure for the China Station, where she served until 1895, the *Mercury*'s torpedo cradles are run out fore and aft at lower deck level. With her sister *Iris* she was the first steel cruiser for the Royal Navy. On trials she made the remarkable speed of 18.57 kts with 7,735 ihp, although designed for only 6,000, and was the fastest warship in existence at the time. Her long slim hull originally had barquentine rig but this was later reduced, as seen. Whereas the *Iris* had a clipper bow, the *Mercury* had a more businesslike plumb bow. Originally despatch vessels, they were later rerated as 2nd class cruisers and rearmed with thirteen 5 in rifled breach-loaders. The *Mercury* was sold for scrap in 1919. (*Public Record Office ADM 176/445*)

Orlando Class

Armoured Cruisers – seven ships, first of class laid down in April 1885. Legend displacement 5,600 tons; length and beam 300 ft (pp) × 56 ft; power 5,500 ihp for 17 kts; principal armament: two 9.2 in and ten 6 in guns, two submerged tubes for 18 in torpedoes; protection: sides, 10 in armour belt (partial), deck 3 in (max).

HMS *Undaunted* (1886). In this 1888 photograph the *Undaunted* still has her original short funnels, which suited these ships well. They were the first armoured or belted cruisers designed without sails (the very first class to dispense with sails were the Merseys: see South Africa in Chapter 6). Developed from the Merseys: the Orlandos were given a 21 per cent increase in beam to accommodate a shallow belt of compound armour 200 ft long: thereby becoming armoured cruisers. However, because they were overweight the belt was too low and, although the *Undaunted* made 19.4 kts on the measured mile, they were generally considered slow ships and relative failures. In consequence, no more armoured cruisers were laid down until 1898. Note the ram bow, which would be a feature of cruisers for a quarter of a century, and the 3 pdrs in the fighting tops. The *Undaunted* was sold for scrap in 1907. (*Public Record Office ADM 176/736*)

2 THE VICTORIAN CRUISER IN THE KAISER'S WAR

The oldest cruisers to see operational service in the First World War were units of the Pallas and Edgar classes. These were ordered under the Naval Defence Act of 7 March 1889 which, *inter alia*, produced forty-two new cruisers of all sizes. The largest of the 1st class protected cruisers, the enormous 14,000 ton Powerful class of 1895, were withdrawn from active service prior to the First World War, but units of the slightly smaller Diadem type did serve. These were weakly armed and protected and were generally kept out of harm's way. The Edgars were a little stronger, but did their best work after conversion to semi-monitors for the ill-starred Dardanelles venture. At a mere 2,100 tons the Pelorus class ships were only one-seventh the size of the Minotaur class of the next period. Such inevitably weak 3rd class protected cruisers had little to offer against Austrian, German or Turkish opposition, but the many 2nd class cruisers were worked hard and were generally successful in operations such as convoy escort or supporting land operations, where their lack of speed was not a handicap. The *Doris* (Eclipse class) made a particular name for herself in operations against Turkish forces. There was a tendency to criticize new classes which were not over-gunned, improvements such as higher sustained speed, longer endurance and better seakeeping being conveniently overlooked. Most of these ships were built with mixed armaments, but the Highflyers introduced a uniform battery of 6 in guns, and a number of earlier ships were similarly rearmed. Some of the smaller Apollos performed valuable work as minelayers.

The new armoured cruisers, all of which fired a heavier weight of metal from their broadside casemates than from their turret-mounted guns, were a disappointment. The Cressys were slow, the Drakes (and Cressys) had too few heavy guns and had the whole of their eight-gun main deck 6 in battery washed out in any kind of seaway, while the Monmouths were weakly protected, were considered under-gunned, also had guns placed too low and had unreliable 6 in turrets. However, these were twins, the first in a British cruiser. None of these twenty big ships were at the Battle of Jutland. Indeed, after 1914 they saw little of the enemy.

The late-Victorian period was not one of rapid change, but some important progress was made. The Edgar class was the first to be designed with armoured casemates, which provided protection for broadside guns, and which remained a feature of large cruisers up to the Duke of Edinburgh class of the next period. Other innovations included QF guns, anti-torpedo nets on larger ships, and triple expansion engines for greater economy and reliability. One result of increased fighting ranges was the deletion of fighting tops from newer designs. Perhaps the most important single development was the introduction of harder and lighter armour of types which remained current to the very end of the cruiser era.

Between 1897 and 1901 several of the older ships featured here had won the battle honours Benin, China or South Africa. They transported troops and supported operations ashore. Although slow by 1914 standards, many of these ships did useful work overseas, particularly while German commerce raiders remained active. They pioneered such innovations as aircraft operating and minelaying. Of the 104 cruisers built in this period, one armoured (the *Bedford*, wrecked), four 1st class, twenty-one 2nd class and twelve 3rd class protected cruisers had been sunk, discarded or relegated to non-operational duties by the outbreak of war.

The end of Queen Victoria's reign, rather than the turn of the century, is a convenient place to end this section.

Apollo Class   2nd Class Protected Cruisers – twenty-one ships, first of class laid down in April 1889. Legend displacement 3,400 tons; length and beam 314 ft × 43 ft; power 7,000 ihp for 18 kts; principal armament: two 6 in and six 4.7 in guns, four 14 in torpedo tubes; protection: 2 in (max) deck.

HMS *Sirius* (1890). The *Sirius* is seen in 1892, about to deploy to become flagship of the South East Coast of America Station. This was the largest class of cruisers ever built for the Royal Navy. About half of them, including the *Sirius* and *Intrepid*, were sheathed for tropical service, which increased displacement by 200 tons to 3,600. Note the mooring spar forward, turtleback forecastle, and poop. In 1915 she participated in operations against German Kamerun (Cameroons), and was later expended as a blockship at Ostend on 23 April 1918. (*Public Record Office ADM 176/644*)

HMS *Naiad* (1890). With her new mine doors and rails clearly visible right aft, the *Naiad* is at Chatham in 1910, where she had been modified as a minelayer. Note the red funnel band. She and six sisters were stripped of their original armament, altered to carry 150 mines, and given a protective battery of six 6 pdrs, four of them on poop. In 1914/15 they formed a homogenous minelaying squadron at Dover. The *Naiad* was sold for scrap in 1922. (*Public Record Office ADM 176/466*)

HMS *Latona* (1890). Seen in 1916, *Latona* is painted in Mediterranean light grey: the tanker behind her is in a simple duotone camouflage. Mines are just visible silhouetted in the waist on the upper deck beneath awnings. Mine rails and doors in the stern are evident. One of the ships modified as a minelayer, she has again been rearmed, this time with four 4 in guns. Sent to the Mediterranean in 1915, it was the *Latona* that laid the mines which sank SMS *Breslau* and badly damaged the German-manned Turkish battlecruiser *Yavus Sultan Selim* (ex-SMS *Goeben*) off Imbros in January 1918. The *Latona* was sold for scrap in 1920. (*Maritime Photo Library 1009*)

HMS *Intrepid* (1891). This is the aftermath of the famous Zeebrugge raid on 23 April 1918, with the *Intrepid*, still reasonably intact, expended as a blockship in the Bruges Canal. German craft are trying vainly to shift her. Beyond her lies her sistership the *Iphigenia*, also used as a blockship. (*Fleet Air Arm Museum CARS I/273*)

Edgar Class 1st Class Protected Cruisers – seven ships, first of the class laid down in June 1889. Legend displacement 7,350 tons; length and beam 387 ft 6 in × 60 ft; power 10,000 ihp for 18 kts; armament: two 9.2 in and ten 6 in guns, four submerged 18 in torpedo tubes; protection: 5 in (max) deck.

HMS *Endymion* (1891). Seen here in Victorian livery, which enhances her balanced profile, the *Endymion* rides at anchor with the booms showing clearly supporting her anti-torpedo nets (a ubiquitous fitting on larger warships of the period). She formed part of Channel Squadron at this time. Unlike their immediate predecessors, the larger and similarly-armed Blakes, all but one of the Edgars saw active service in the First World War. They exceeded their designed speed in service and were generally successful. The *Endymion* was sold for scrap in 1920. (*Plymouth Naval Base Museum*)

HMS *Grafton* (1892). This rare snapshot shows the *Grafton* passing Imbros with another cruiser, a monitor and escorts before entering the Dardanelles. Her mainmast has been considerably shortened and she has an AA gun right aft. She remained in Middle East theatres throughout the war, and later served in the Black Sea as part of the force supporting the White Russians. Together with the *Edgar*, *Endymion* and *Theseus*, the *Grafton* had exchanged her two 9.2 in guns for 6 in, to achieve a uniform battery of twelve guns. They had also been fitted with net-sweeping gallows on the bows and huge anti-torpedo bulges, being known at the time as blister ships. Her bulges enabled the *Grafton* to survive a torpedo hit amidships in June 1917. In late 1917 she engaged Turkish forces at Gaza in support of General Allenby. The *Grafton* was sold for scrap in 1920. (*Fleet Air Arm Museum CARS G/133*)

HMS *Theseus* (1892). Laid up in 1919/20, possibly in the Black Sea, where she had served, the *Theseus* displays all the modifications made to four of this class for the Dardanelles Campaign. The curved top of the huge protective bulge creates the illusion of the ship listing to starboard. During active service she wore a distinctive band on each funnel. On 21 October 1915, with the *Doris*, the *Theseus* bombarded barracks at Dedeagatch. She was sold for scrap in 1921. (*National Maritime Museum N29304*)

Crescent Class   1st Class Protected Cruisers – two ships, first of the class laid down in January 1890. Legend displacement 7,700 tons; length and beam 38 7ft 6 in × 60 ft 9 in; power 10,000 ihp for 18 kts; armament: one 9.2 in and twelve 6 in guns, four submerged 18 in torpedo tubes; protection: 5 in (max) deck.

HMS *Royal Arthur* (1891). In this very early view, which probably dates from 1897, no anti-torpedo nets are fitted. The two ships of this class appear to have been the last to feature decorative scrollwork on their bows. Developed from the Edgars, the Crescents were sheathed for tropical service, increasing their displacement. The forward 9.2 in gun was replaced by two sided 6 in and the forecastle was raised one deck for improved seakeeping, which made these guns easier to work. Neither ship saw active service after the first year of the war. The *Royal Arthur* was sold for scrap in 1921. (*Plymouth Naval Base Museum*)

Astraea Class   2nd Class Protected Cruisers – eight ships, first laid down in August 1890. Legend displacement 4,360 tons; length and beam 339 ft 6 in × 49 ft 6 in; power 7,500 ihp for 18 kts; principal armament: two 6 in and eight 4.7 in guns, four 18 in torpedo tubes; protection: 2 in deck.

HMS *Charybdis* (1893). Part of the Channel Squadron between 1896 and 1898, the *Charybdis* displays the typical Victorian cruiser profile. All the two-funnel classes (and similarly all the three-funnel classes) of the era were of broadly similar appearance. Light 6 pdrs are spaced between the 4.7 in guns on the broadside, all trained outboard. The Astraeas were enlarged Apollos with higher freeboard amidships for better seakeeping. (*Plymouth Naval Base Museum*)

HMS *Charybdis*. Here the *Charybdis* is escorting one of the convoys carrying the British Expeditionary Force across the English Channel in August 1914. There appears to be a light gun on the forecastle ahead of No. one 6 in. Otherwise, except for the addition of a spotting top on the foremast, there is little evidence of alterations in the intervening years. The *Charybdis* was leased for mercantile use in 1918 and sold for scrap 1922. (*National Maritime Museum*)

Eclipse Class 2nd Class Protected Cruisers – nine ships, first laid down in December 1893. Legend displacement 5,600 tons; length and beam 373 ft × 53 ft 6 in; power 9,600 ihp for 19.5 kts; principal armament: five 6 in, six 4.7 in and eight 12 pdr (3 in) guns, three 18 in torpedo tubes (two submerged); protection: 3 in (max) deck.

HMS *Eclipse* (1894). This May 1897 official portrait captures the *Eclipse* at South Railway Jetty, Portsmouth, with Semaphore Tower in the background. She is about to sail to become flagship of the East Indies Station, and is painted in the station colours: white with buff masts and funnels. There are guns in fighting tops, and the item at the head of the mainmast is a set of semaphore arms. Her funnel caps are a unique identifying feature. These ships were enlarged Astraeas. The *Eclipse* was sold for scrap 1921. (*Public Record Office ADM 176/223*)

HMS *Isis* (1896). Wearing the new Edwardian 'crabfat' (i.e. grey) livery, introduced at the beginning of that reign, and with distinguishing funnel bands, the *Isis* is seen in about 1912. She has windsails in place of ventilation cowls, and there are no guns in the fighting tops. The turtleback forecastle was a distinctive feature of this class. The *Isis* was sold for scrap in 1920. (*Ian Allan/Science Museum/Science & Society S1051*)

HMS *Talbot* (1895). With HMS *Challenger* in the background, the *Talbot* is anchored off the coast of German East Africa in 1916. Both ships have windsails rigged for ventilation. She was the only ship in the class without fighting tops. On 4 September she took part, with the *Challenger* and *Hyacinth*, in the capture of Dar es Salaam. The *Talbot* was sold for scrap in 1921. (*Fleet Air Arm Museum CARS C/214*)

HMS *Minerva* (1895). In this January 1915 image the *Minerva* is painted in a complicated overall camouflage scheme. There are 3 pdr guns in the bridge wings, and 'dodgers' (windproof canvas screens) have been rigged on the forward spotting top and aft fighting top. Except for the *Eclipse* the whole class had been rearmed between 1902 and 1904 with eleven 6 in guns. The *Minerva* saw much service in Middle Eastern waters during the first half of the First World War, and was sold for scrap in 1920. (*Maritime Photo Library 1029*)

Arrogant Class 2nd Class Protected Cruisers (Fleet Rams) – four ships, first laid down in June 1895. Legend displacement 5,750 tons; length and beam 342 f × 57 ft 6 in; power 10,000 ihp for 19 kts; principal armament: four 6 in, six 4.7 in and eight 12 pdr guns three 18 in torpedo tubes (two submerged); protection sides (forward, supporting ram) 2 in, 3 in (max) deck.

HMS *Vindictive* (1897). Photographed after her return from the St George's Day raid on Zeebrugge, her upperworks are riddled but the hull, which her position alongside the mole had protected, is virtually unscratched. For the raid on 23 April 1918 her armament had been radically changed. Of her original outfit she retained two 6 in each side on the upper deck. In addition, Admiral Keyes ordered her to carry an 11 in howitzer on the quarterdeck, two 7.5 in howitzers and two large fixed 'flamenwerfers', two pom-poms (automatic 40 mm/2 pdr cannon, primarily for AA work) and six Lewis light machine-guns in the foretop, plus three pom-poms, ten Lewis and four batteries of Stokes mortars on the port side. The mainmast has been removed, and numerous portable gangways and bridges, plus a false deck, fitted. The *Vindictive* returned from Zeebrugge but she was expended as a blockship at Ostend on 10 May. (*The Liddle Collection/University of Leeds*)

Diadem Class 1st Class Protected Cruisers – four ships, first laid down in December 1895. Legend displacement 11,000 tons; length and beam 462 ft 6 in × 69 ft; power 16,500 ihp for 20.25 kts; principal armament: sixteen 6 in and fourteen 12 pdr guns, three 18 in torpedo tubes (two submerged); protection: 4 in (max) deck.

HMS *Europa* (1897). Lying at Mudros in 1917, where she was flagship between 1915 and 1919, the *Europa* is being camouflaged. On her hull there are false bow and stern waves, together with a light patch above the hawse hole. In this view the funnels are in the process of being camouflaged, with painters in position on the two centre stacks. There is also camouflage on the foremast. On 15 September 1899 she became one of the first three Royal Navy ships to carry operational wireless. The huge hulls, with their 32 ft freeboard forward, made for good seakeeping, but the total lack of side armour made them enormous and vulnerable targets. The *Europa* was sold for mercantile use in 1920. (*Maritime Photo Library 937*)

Pelorus Class   3rd Class Protected Cruisers – eleven ships, first laid down in March 1890. Legend displacement 2,135 tons; length and beam 313 ft 6 in × 36 ft 6 in; power 5,000 ihp for 18.5 kts; principal armament: eight 4 in guns, two 14 in torpedo tubes; protection: 2 in (max) deck.

HMS *Pegasus* (1897). This sad scene shows the *Pegasus* beached off Zanzibar, down by bows and listing to starboard. Because an early-warning system failed, she had been surprised and disabled by the German light cruiser SMS *Königsberg* on 20 September 1914. There are collapsed awnings above upper deck. These small cruisers were the successors to the Pallas class (see New Zealand in Chapter 6). (*Maritime Photo Library 1107*)

HMS *Pomone* (1897). At the end of her working life the little *Pomone* is being towed away from the River Dart to the breaker's yard. In her youth she was the fastest of the Pelorus class, reaching a speed of 20.2 kts on trials. After brief service in the East Indies she was laid up for six years because of her troublesome Blechynden boilers, before becoming harbour training ship to Britannia Royal Naval College at Dartmouth in about January 1910. She remained there until being sold for scrap in 1922. (*Royal Navy*)

Ariadne Class 1st Class Protected Cruisers – four ships, first laid down in October 1896. Legend displacement 11,000 tons; length and beam 462 ft 6 in × 69 ft 6 in; power 18,000 ihp for 20.75 kts; principal armament: sixteen 6 in and fourteen 12 pdr guns, three 18 in torpedo tubes (two submerged); protection: 4 in (max) deck.

HMS *Ariadne* (1898). As flagship of the North America and West Indies Station, she is at Halifax, Nova Scotia, in about 1904. She is riding high, presumably awaiting her 1,900 tons of coal, with what appears to be green boot topping exposed. The close-stowing anchors could not be drawn into the hawse holes, and were instead secured by chains to the ship's sides either horizontally or vertically (as here). White bands on Victorian livery at both forecastle and upper deck levels were not common. The *Ariadne* made 21.5 kts on trials, the fastest of class. She was torpedoed and sunk by *UC65* on 26 July 1917. (*Notman Studio/National Archives of Canada PA-28470*)

HMS *Argonaut* (1898). Serving as a unit of 9 CS in 1915, she is wearing partial camouflage. This is confined to light hull panels fore and aft, with sloping ends, and panels, similar to those seen on the *Europa*, on the funnels. The white ensign appears to have been retouched. The *Argonaut* was sold for scrap in 1920. (*Maritime Photo Library 929*)

HMS *Amphitrite* (1898). Converted to a minelayer in 1916/17, in this 1918 view the *Amphitrite* displays a complicated multi-colour dazzle scheme based on designs of marine artist Norman Wilkinson. All casemates appear to be empty, but six 6 in guns have been resited on the forecastle deck abreast the funnels. Note the shortened topmasts. The *Amphitrite* was sold for scrap in 1920. (*Maritime Photo Library 926*)

Highflyer Class   2nd Class Protected Cruisers – three ships, first laid down in January 1897. Legend displacement 5,600 tons; length and beam 372 ft × 54 ft; power 10,000 ihp for 20 kts; principal armament: eleven 6 in and nine 12 pdr guns, two submerged 18 in torpedo tubes; protection: 3 in (max) deck.

HMS *Hyacinth* (1898). Riding off Simon's Town on 22 September 1913, at the time of the visit of the magnificent UK-built Japanese battlecruiser *Kongo*, the *Hyacinth*'s tropical white hull contrasts starkly with the latter's dark grey. HIJMS *Kongo* is *en route* to Japan from the Vickers shipyard at Barrow. In January 1915 the *Hyacinth* joined the watch for the German light cruiser *Königsberg*. Later, she sank two German supply ships off German East Africa. This class was a natural progression from the Eclipses. The *Hyacinth* was sold for scrap in 1923. (*Simon's Town Museum*)

HMS *Highflyer* (1898). With SS *Marmora* in the background in 1916, the *Highflyer* is in harbour while operating off the Cape Verde Islands and West Africa. On 26 August 1914 she surprised and sank the armed merchant cruiser *Kaiser Wilhelm der Grosse* coaling between two colliers off Rio de Oro. Apart from the two Sentinel class scouts, these were the last cruisers to feature a turtleback forecastle deck. The *Highflyer* was the last Victorian cruiser in active commission, paying off from the East Indies Station for scrap in 1921. (*Maritime Photo Library 1041*)

Cressy Class Armoured Cruisers – six ships, first laid down in July 1898. Legend displacement 12,000 tons; length and beam 472 ft × 69 ft 6 in; power 21,000 ihp for 21 kts; principal armament: two 9.2 in, twelve 6 in and twelve 12 pdr guns, two submerged 18 in torpedo tubes; protection: sides 6 in (max) armour belt (partial), 3 in (max) deck.

HMS *Aboukir* (1900). At Portsmouth in about 1902, the *Aboukir* has the then-customary W/T gaff on the mainmast. The Cressys were the first armoured cruisers since the Orlandos of 1885, and were basically better-armed belted Diadems. They had a belt of Krupp cemented steel 6 in armour 231 ft long and 11.5 ft deep, closed with 5 in bulkheads and continued to bow by 2 in plates. This was much thinner and lighter than the old compound armour of similar resistance. The whole class was sheathed with teak and copper for tropical service, because anti-fouling compounds were then inadequate. With her sisters *Cressy* and *Hogue* (see next plate), she was sunk by *U9* on 22 September 1914 in a terrible demonstration of the power of the submarine. (*Royal Navy*)

HMS *Hogue* (1900). In this view, dated 1912, she is wearing standard funnel bands. There is a range drum on the fore spotting top and, with the rest of the class, she had an admiral's stern walk. The fastest ship of her class, the *Hogue* achieved 22.4 kts on trials. As part of the 7th Cruiser Squadron she towed in the damaged *Arethusa* after the Battle of Heligoland Bight on 28 August 1914. Later, she was sunk with her sisters *Aboukir* (see previous plate) and *Cressy*. (*Royal Marines Museum*)

HMS *Bacchante* (1901). Thought to be at Mudros, the *Bacchante* has white turrets, a false bow wave and light grey upperworks. The many boats alongside could indicate disembarkation of troops, in which she was involved in July and December 1915. She was heavily involved in bombarding Turkish positions throughout most of 1915 and again in 1916. On 6 August, during the Suvla Operation, the *Bacchante* led the preparatory bombardment in support of the Anzac assault on Lone Pine Hill. The *Bacchante* was sold for scrap in 1920. (*Royal Naval Museum Portsmouth*)

HMS *Euryalus* (1901). Photographed during the Dardanelles Campaign (this image is dated 1915/16), the *Euryalus* has no false bow wave. The 3 pdrs on the roofs of the two turrets are at a high angle, and may be AA. There are no 6 in guns in the midships main deck casemates. A large MV is alongside to port. On 5 March 1915 she began the bombardment of the Smyrna forts. There, fire from her 9.2s exploded two magazines at Fort Yeni Kale and destroyed a 24 cm gun. The *Euryalus* was sold for scrap in 1920. (*National Maritime Museum C9169/C*)

Opposite, top: HMS *Leviathan* (1901). The *Leviathan* is on speed trials on the Skelmorlie measured mile in 1903, with windsails rigged for ventilating the machinery spaces. No guns are fitted and none of the heavier ship's boats are carried. The Drakes, which were enlarged Cressys, were fast ships and good steamers, 25 kts being available and high speeds sustainable for long periods. (*Business Records Centre, University of Glasgow*)

Opposite, bottom: HMS *Leviathan.* A member of 6 CS, the *Leviathan* is under way off Halifax in mid-1915. She displays a false bow wave and dazzle-painted funnels, and the topmasts have been shortened. All 6 in guns are trained outboard. Long before this the main deck 12 pdr embrasures forward were plated over in the whole class. The *Leviathan* was sold for scrap in 1920. (*J. R. Curry/National Archives of Canada PA-112341*)

Drake Class Armoured Cruisers – four ships, first laid down in April 1899. Legend displacement 14,150 tons; length and beam 533 ft 6 in × 71 ft 4 in; power 30,000 ihp for 23 kts; principal armament: two 9.2 in, sixteen 6 in and fourteen 12 pdr guns, two submerged 18 in torpedo tubes; protection: sides, 6 in (max) belt (partial), deck 2.5 in (max).

HMS *Good Hope* (1901). Seen here leaving Portsmouth as flagship of the 1st Cruiser Squadron, she is wearing, among her oversized flags, that of a rear-admiral. The lower of the double-tiered 12 pdrs in the bow proved unworkable in a seaway and were later plated over. The main deck 6 in guns were also difficult to work and are not rigged in the lower midships casemates. The *Good Hope* wore the flag of RAd Sir Christopher Cradock when sunk by SMS *Scharnhorst* and *Gneisenau* at the Battle of Coronel on 1 November 1914. (*Royal Marines Museum*)

Monmouth Class   Armoured Cruisers – ten ships, first laid down in August 1899. Legend displacement 9,800 tons; length and beam 463 ft 6 in × 66 ft; power 22,000 ihp for 23 kts; principal armament: fourteen 6 in and ten 12 pdr guns, two submerged 18 in torpedo tubes; protection: sides, 4 in (max) belt (partial), deck 2 in (max).

HMS *Monmouth* (1901). On builder's trials on the Clyde in Victorian livery on a murky day at the end of 1903, as yet the *Monmouth* has no guns or large ship's boats. The customary W/T gaff is fitted. Scaled-down Drakes, with their fine underwater lines and 4 in belts, the Monmouths were fastest and weakest of the armoured cruisers. The *Monmouth* was sunk at the Battle of Coronel on 1 November 1914. (*National Maritime Museum 59/2105*)

HMS *Cornwall* (1902). This peaceful interlude is at Simon's Town in April 1915, when the *Cornwall* was *en route* to the Middle East after a post-action refit at Avonmouth. Four months later she bombarded Turkish positions during the Dardanelles Campaign. Earlier, with the *Glasgow*, she sank SMS *Leipzig* at the Battle of the Falkland Islands on 8 December 1914. (*Simon's Town Museum*)

HMS *Cornwall*. Laid up in the River Tamar in about 1919, the *Cornwall* is serving as a stationary tender to HMS *Vivid*. Windsails are in evidence, but the six 6 in guns from the main deck, which were at one stage resited on the upper deck, have been landed. Also, there are no light guns or large ship's boats. The *Cornwall* was sold for scrap in 1920. (*Ian Allan / Science Museum / Science & Society S1159*)

HMS *Suffolk* (1903). The unusual two-tone paint scheme she is wearing while lying off Halifax, possibly in April 1915, may be an earlier version of the medium green hull and medium light blue upperworks later said to have been worn by the light cruiser *Carysfort*. The *Suffolk* made 24.7 kts on trials, but on 6 August 1914, when she came upon SMS *Karlsruhe* coaling, the German light cruiser, which made 28.5 kts on trials, was able to evade action. In January 1918 the *Suffolk* arrived at Vladivostok for operations against the Bolsheviks. The *Suffolk* was sold for scrap in 1920. (*J. McLaughlan/Public Archives of Canada PA-112433*)

HMS *Kent* (1901). Riding at anchor off Esquimalt, British Columbia, in June 1915, after over six months of action and strenuous operations, the *Kent* is awaiting refit. There are men working at the top of the third funnel. She sank SMS *Nürnberg* at the Battle of the Falkland Islands on 8 December 1914, when a speed of over 25 kts was claimed. Later, she supported the *Glasgow* in the destruction of the *Dresden* on 14 March 1915. The *Kent* was sold for scrap in 1920. (*Canadian Patent & Copyright Office/Public Archives of Canada PA30231*)

HMS *Berwick* (1902). The backdrop of this rare portrait is probably Eastern Canada in 1918. In common with other ocean escort cruisers she wears full dazzle. The six 6 in guns have been removed from the main deck casemates and at least four are now in open shields in the waist on the upper deck. Also, in common with others of the class by this date, her forward 12 pdr embrasures are plated over. In September 1914 the *Berwick* captured several German prizes, including the naval auxiliary *Spreewald*. The *Berwick* was sold for scrap in 1920. (*Dept of National Defence Collection/National Archives of Canada PA-205131*)

HMS *Donegal* (1902). In this 1918 aerial view the *Donegal* is painted in the full dazzle of an ocean escort. As was normal, the main deck 6 in guns have been resited on upper deck and, except for a shortened main topmast, she is similar to the *Berwick*. Some new plating aft has not been painted to match. In June 1917 she joined the North America & West Indies Station, which provided the cruisers that escorted transatlantic convoys. The *Donegal* was sold for scrap in 1920. (*J.J. Colledge*)

HMS *Cumberland* (1902). The *Cumberland* was one of the few big cruisers to be given seagoing duties after the war. Painted in post-war overall grey, she served as a training cruiser between 1919 and 1920, as seen here. Her armament had been reduced to eight 6 in and there appear to be no light guns. The upper bridge has been glazed. During 1914/15 the *Cumberland* was heavily engaged in the conquest of German Kamerun (Cameroons). The *Cumberland* was sold for scrap in 1921. (*National Maritime Museum N1149*)

Challenger Class 2nd Class Protected Cruisers – two ships, first laid down in December 1900. Legend displacement 5,915 tons; length and beam 376 ft × 56 ft; power 12,500 ihp for 21 kts; principal armament: eleven 6 in and nine 12 pdr guns, two submerged 18 in torpedo tubes; protection: 3 in (max) deck.

HMS *Challenger* (1902). This interesting 1907 aerial view, overlooking Auckland Dock in New Zealand, reveals many details. This class lacked the prominent ventilation cowls of the similar Highflyers, and the forecastle deck, which is slightly cut away to provide a degree of end-on fire for Nos two and three 6 in guns, is flat. She has modern stockless anchors, although the second is secured by the old method. This was the last class of cruiser laid down in the Victorian era. The *Challenger* was sold for scrap in 1920. (*Plymouth Naval Base Museum*)

3 FROM EDWARD VII TO THE FIRST WORLD WAR AND BEYOND

It is among the ships laid down in this period that the major players in the First World War are to be found. The first new cruisers were the six ships of the Devonshire class. These introduced the 7.5 in gun, firing a 200 lb shell. Also, they had, for the first time, four main armament turrets and a cutaway forecastle deck to allow the wing turrets axial fire. The design marked a halfway point between the lightly armed Victorian armoured cruisers and the last three classes, which were almost second-class battleships. The last of these introduced to cruisers twin turrets for big guns. There were several other technical developments during this period, a landmark being the installation of turbine machinery experimentally for the first time in HMS *Amethyst*, one of the little Gems. The first class to be fitted with turbines was the 1908 Boadicea class of scout cruisers. This type had evolved to match the sea speed of the latest torpedo boat destroyers, which the older classes could neither support nor counter. There followed twenty-one ships of the five classes of the Town group. The first two were 25–26 knot 2nd class protected cruisers, but the following Chathams had a

thin and narrow armour belt, although this was not sufficiently extensive for them to be classed as armoured cruisers. The Bristols of 1909 had a mixed armament, but the remainder had a uniform main armament of 6 in or 5.5 in guns.

Destroyer speeds continued to increase, as did those of capital ships, and 25 knots became inadequate. This led to the introduction of the Arethusa class of 1913, also with a mixed main armament of 6 in and 4 in guns. Their most notable feature was their unprecedented speed of 28.5 knots, which enabled them to keep station with the latest large destroyers. Another 1913 innovation was a major rationalization of the multitude of cruiser types. All were swept away and replaced by only two categories: Cruisers and Light Cruisers. The former comprised those ships with armour at least 4 in thick and the latter the more lightly protected classes. Both armament and tonnage were irrelevant to classification. The eight Arethusas, together with the succeeding thirty-six ships of the C and D classes, were all launched by 1919 and were all of less than 5,000 tons: too small for fleet operations outside the North Sea or for trade protection duties worldwide. The Calliope class of 1914 introduced geared turbines and the Centaurs of 1916 were the first to have an all-centreline main armament. The Ceres class was a milestone design which introduced into cruiser service a superfiring gun in B position.

To fill the trade protection rôle the splendid large light cruisers of the Hawkins class were introduced, although none entered service as a cruiser in the First World War. Armed with 7.5 in guns and capable of 30 knots, they were able, at some 10,000 tons, to carry sufficient fuel to ply the world's oceans. Their very existence was of unforeseen significance, as will be shown in the next chapter. They were followed by the very fast Emeralds, the building of both these classes being prompted by false reports of powerful German ships.

The sudden return to peace resulted in completion of the last of the Hawkins class and the Es being delayed until after the signing of the Washington Naval Treaty of 1922. Despite disappointment with the twin 6 in turret in the Victorian Monmouth class, a modern pattern twin turret was installed in the new Enterprise. It proved successful and was adapted for use as the secondary armament of the new Nelson class battleships and the main armament of the next three classes of light cruisers. The Enterprise also carried the prototype director control tower (DCT). The development of this is outlined in the Appendix.

One of the most important technical developments of this period was the introduction of the gunnery director, which made possible accurate fire over much greater ranges. Except for the scouts, all modern light cruisers were so fitted, but only a few of the cruisers. Tripod masts also appeared. These reduced vibration in the spotting top and were essential supports for aloft directors. Anti-aircraft guns were fitted in increasing numbers to all cruisers likely to be operating within range of enemy aircraft, including Victorian ships. AA positions were designed into newer classes. Camouflage began to be applied to old and new ships alike from the very beginning of the war. Later, in an attempt to counter the submarine threat, many ships were dazzle-painted, in order to deceive U-boat crews as to a ship's heading. Some ships were fitted with baffles on masts and funnels to render range-taking more difficult. Unfortunately, although these were effective with coincidence rangefinders, as used by the Royal Navy, the Germans used stereoscopic instruments which were not affected. As a result of the unpleasant lessons of the Battle of Coronel the main deck 6 in guns on larger cruisers were moved to higher decks during refits. In order to reduce wetness, designs became cleaner, with fewer openings and excrescences on the hull side, especially forward.

Post-war changes were few. Larger but fewer searchlights were fitted. The 4 in became the standard heavy AA gun, and more ships received pom-poms. To comply with international treaties, the Hawkins class was demilitarized in the 1930s, but they were later rearmed and, with the Es, went on to serve in the Second World War. The Effingham received 6 in guns, giving her the perhaps unique distinction of being a light cruiser when new, a heavy cruiser in popular parlance under the terms of the 1930 London Treaty, and then a light cruiser again under the terms of the same treaty.

Wartime losses were, sadly, inevitable, but 1914 brought new and unknown risks. The torpedoing of the three Cressys was a new lesson harshly learnt, but hardly avoidable in the circumstances. To the *Cassandra* went the dubious distinction of being mined after the war with Germany had ended. During the war the post-dreadnought ships were worked hard and were generally successful, although the Towns were sometimes embarrassed by a lack of speed, and the war at sea could not have been won without them.

During the late 1930s and early 1940s several Cs and the *Delhi* were converted into invaluable AA ships. No fewer than three Caledons, all five Ceres class and two Danaes saw active service in both world wars. Until D-Day bombardments gave some a new lease of life in 1944, the pre-Washington Treaty designs were fit for nothing more than convoy escort in the Second World War.

Devonshire Class Armoured Cruisers – six ships, first laid down in March 1902. Legend displacement 10,850 tons; length and beam 473 ft 6 in × 69 ft 6 in; power 21,000 ihp for 22.25 kts; principal armament: four 7.5 in six 6 in and two 12 pdr guns, two submerged 18 in torpedo tubes; protection: sides, 6 in (max) belt (partial), deck 2 in (max).

HMS *Carnarvon* (1903). Seen here off Plymouth prior to the First World War, this handsome ship is flying a rear-admiral's flag. The *Carnarvon* fought Admiral von Spee's heavy ships at the Battle of the Falkland Islands in December 1914, firing 85 rounds of 7.5 in at the sinking SMS *Scharnhorst* and later at the *Gneisenau*. The latter's survivors claimed that the *Carnarvon*'s fire was more effective than that of the battlecruisers, many of whose 12 in shells passed through the German cruiser without exploding. Post-war, she served as a seagoing training cruiser until 1921. The Devonshires were the first new class laid down in the Edwardian era, and began the trend towards multi-turreted main armament. The *Carnarvon* was sold for scrap in 1921. (*Plymouth Naval Base Museum*)

HMS *Hampshire* (1903). This rare photograph, taken at Scapa Flow in early 1916, is believed to be the last image of the *Hampshire*. It clearly shows that the 6 in guns from main deck have been resited on upper deck, a modification applied to the whole class. Her main topmast has been reduced to a stump. She survived the Battle of Jutland but, sadly, she is most widely remembered as the ship in which Lord Kitchener met his death, when she was mined off West Orkney on 5 June 1916, while setting out on her second trip to Russia. Unfortunately, the fore part of the ship is off camera. (*National Maritime Museum N16832*)

HMS *Devonshire* (1904). Her ocean escort paint scheme, as seen in this rare 1918 photograph, is almost too subdued to be called dazzle. There are two light colours, divided on the hull into rectangular panels, overlaid with dark areas containing no verticals. Even the *Devonshire*'s spotting tops are so treated. During one transatlantic convoy she towed SS *Mahsud* across the Atlantic for five days. The *Devonshire* was sold for scrap in 1921. (*Royal Naval Museum Portsmouth*)

HMS *Roxburgh* (1904). Off Plymouth in late 1918, and wearing full dazzle, the *Roxburgh* displays on her first funnel the red star awarded for ramming and sinking *U89* north of Ireland on 12 February 1918. This was full retribution for being torpedoed by *U38* on 20 June 1915. Only she and the *Argyll* had sloping funnel tops. A pair of single 6 in guns in shields can be seen in her waist. She had the honour of escorting the first regular convoy from Hampton Roads, Virginia, on 24 May 1917. The fastest of the Devonshires she made over 23.6 kts on trials. However, the class became poor steamers as they aged. The *Roxburgh* was sold for scrap in 1921. (© *Tom Molland*)

HMS *Antrim* (1903). This 1922 photograph shows the *Antrim* in her final form. Although she retains all ten heavy guns, most light guns have been landed. She had paid off at the end of 1917 and completed a major refit to equip her as a W/T trials ship: there are experimental aerials ahead of the second funnel. In 1921 Asdic was fitted and she conducted the first trials. Later, accommodation for trainees was added aft of 'A' turret, which could then no longer train. The *Antrim* was the last armoured cruiser to survive in service, becoming a seagoing tender to the Signals School in April 1922 and being sold for disposal on 19 December, less than a year before the design of the new 8 in County class was being settled. (*Royal Naval Museum Portsmouth*)

Topaze Class   3rd Class Protected Cruisers – four ships, first laid down in August 1902. Legend displacement 3,000 tons; length and beam 373 ft 9 in × 40 ft; power 9,800 ihp for 21.75 kts; principal armament: twelve 4 in guns, two 18 in torpedo tubes; protection: 2 in deck.

HMS *Topaze* (1903). This builder's photograph shows the *Topaze* as completed in 1904. These were the last of the 3rd class cruisers, and were better ships all round than the previous Pelorus class, to which they bore little resemblance. However, they were too slow for their time, slower even than the big armoured cruisers, and therefore tactically limited. Because of this, four additional ships were cancelled. The flair of the hull is cut away fore and aft to allow a degree of end-on fire for the first and last pairs of broadside 4 in guns. The searchlight over the conning tower forward is interesting. The *Topaze* was sold for scrap in 1921. (*Cammell Laird Archives/Wirral Museum*)

HMS *Amethyst* (1903). On a typical North Sea day in about 1909 the *Amethyst* is blowing off surplus steam in a stiff breeze from the port bow. Wireless communication is now by high-mounted aerials and there are semaphore sets in the bridge wings. The *Amethyst* is most famous for being the first British cruiser with turbine machinery. This produced 12,000 shp for 22.5 kts. The *Amethyst* was sold for scrap in 1920. (*National Maritime Museum*)

Duke of Edinburgh Class Armoured Cruisers – two ships, first laid down in February 1903. Legend displacement 13,550 tons (actually about 12,600); length and beam 505 ft 6 in × 73 ft 6 in; power 23,000 ihp for 23 kts; principal armament: six 9.2 in and ten 6 in guns, three submerged 18 in torpedo tubes; protection: sides, 6 in (max) belt, deck 1.5 in (max).

HMS *Black Prince* (1904). In this interesting photograph the *Black Prince* is seen with six of her 6 in guns in open shields on the upper deck, to where they had been moved in June 1915. The two ships of this class originally had an armoured battery of ten 6 in guns on the main deck, as in the contemporary King Edward VII class battleships, but these proved impossible to work in a seaway and the class was deemed a failure. However, after modification they had a more useful secondary armament than the Warriors. The *Black Prince* was sunk at the Battle of Jutland in the early morning of 1 June 1916. (*National Maritime Museum N16668*)

HMS *Duke of Edinburgh* (1904). At the yard of shipbreakers Hughes Bolckow, to whom she had been sold in 1920, the *Duke of Edinburgh* is still wearing dazzle camouflage. Although all 9.2 in turrets remain, the single 6 in, which had earlier been moved from the main deck to the upper deck amidships, have gone. The tripod foremast was a post-Jutland addition. In August 1914 she captured the German steamer *Altair* in the Red Sea. Two months later, on 10 November, she bombarded Turkish positions at Sheikh Sa'id in Southern Arabia. The *Duke of Edinburgh* survived the Battle of Jutland and later became an ocean escort for transatlantic convoys. (*Copyright*)

Sentinal Class   Scout Cruisers – two ships, first laid down in June 1903. Legend displacement 2,880 tons; length and beam 381 ft × 40 ft; power 17,000 ihp for 25 kts; principal armament: ten 12 pdr guns, two 18 in torpedo tubes; protection: 2 in (max) deck.

HMS *Sentinel* (1904). Proceeding out of Devonport Dockyard in about 1911, the *Sentinel* displays distinguishing funnel bands typical of the period. This was the first class of scout cruisers, designed to have the speed to lead flotillas of the latest fast destroyers. Four pairs of ships were designed by private contractors, all basically similar but differing in detail. The main feature of the *Sentinel* was the old-fashioned turtleback forecastle deck. She was sold for scrap in 1923. (*Plymouth Naval Base Museum*)

Pathfinder Class Scout Cruisers – two ships, first laid down in August 1903. Legend displacement 2,940 tons; length and beam 379 ft × 38 ft 6 in; power 16,500 ihp for 25 kts; principal armament: ten 12 pdr guns, two 18 in torpedo tubes; protection: sides, 2 in belt (partial), deck 1.5 in (max).

HMS *Pathfinder* (1904). Building up speed on trials in 1905, the *Pathfinder* is making very modest waves. With their funnels amidships these ships had a similar profile to the Topaze class, but, lacking a mainmast, the W/T gaff was forward. The main feature of this pair was the provision of modest side protection. The *Pathfinder* had the dubious distinction of becoming, on 5 September 1914, the first warship lost to submarine attack. (*Cammell Laird Archives/Wirral Museum*)

Forward Class Scout Cruisers – two ships, first laid down October 1903. Legend displacement 2,860 tons; length and beam 379 ft × 39 ft 3 in; power 16,500 ihp for 25 kts; principal armament: ten 12 pdr guns, two 18 in torpedo tubes; protection: sides, 2 in (max) belt (partial), deck 0.63 in (max) (partial).

HMS *Forward* (1904). The *Forward* is at anchor in the Mediterranean theatre in about 1917, with her boarding ladder down and still wearing a funnel band. She has been rearmed with nine 4 in plus one 3 in AA. The 4 in guns are paired, port and starboard, except for the single centre-line gun on the raised poop. Aft of this is at least one pom-pom. She was sold for scrap in 1921. (*National Maritime Museum D1715*)

Warrior Class Armoured Cruisers – four ships, first laid down in November 1903. Legend displacement 13,550 tons; length and beam 505 ft 6 in × 73 ft 6 in; power 23,000 ihp for 23 kts; principal armament: six 9.2 in and four 7.5 in guns, three submerged 18 in torpedo tubes; protection: sides, 6 in (max) belt, deck 1.5 in (max).

HMS *Cochrane* (1905). Just out of refit and off Plymouth on 29 October 1917, the *Cochrane* displays her new tall tripod foremast. There is a 3 in AA gun under canvas on the quarterdeck. Although considered the best large cruisers of the pre-Dreadnought era, the Warriors were particularly weak in anti-flotilla craft defence, having no guns between ultra-light 3 pdrs and the slow-firing 7.5 in. (*Royal Navy*)

HMS *Cochrane*. Among the ice floes in Pechenga Bay (Petsamo), the *Cochrane* is seen during the summer of 1918. She has been fitted for, but not with, a gunnery director on the foremast, as the empty circular platform below the spotting top testifies. The topmast has been moved from the fore to the main. She had arrived at Murmansk on 7 March to assist with the defence of the Kola Inlet against the advancing Germans. The *Cochrane* was wrecked in the Mersey on her return home on 14 November 1918, three days after the Armistice. (*Liddle Collection / University of Leeds*)

HMS *Achilles* (1905). The *Achilles* is at anchor off New York, where she arrived on 10 November 1918. The striking dazzle camouflage contains no verticals, in order to make range and bearing estimation more difficult. The owner of the photograph, who served on her at the time, recalled that the pattern included various pinks and other surprising colours. The *Achilles* has

received a gunnery director, on the platform before the tripod foremast. With the armed boarding vessel *Dundee*, she sank the commerce raider SMS *Leopard* on 16 March 1917, and was the only member of the class to survive to be scrapped – in 1920. (*V. Ballard via author*)

Adventure Class Scout Cruisers – two ships, first laid down in January 1904. Legend displacement 2,640 tons; length and beam 395 ft 6 in × 38 ft 3 in; power 16,000 ihp for 25 kts; principal armament: ten 12 pdr guns, two 18 in torpedo tubes; protection: 2 in (max) deck.

HMS *Attentive* (1904). This photograph dates from about late 1915, and the *Attentive* is seen with a bomb-laden Short 184 floatplane taxying in the foreground. The *Attentive* had been bombed and damaged by German aircraft off Ostend on 7 September 1915. She later joined HMS *Cochrane* at Murmansk in support of White Russians. On 1 August 1918 she engaged the Bolshevik fort at Mudyugski, when she survived being hit by a 6 in shell. The two ships of this class were the first to feature a cutaway bow. They were rearmed pre-war with nine 4 in plus one 3 in AA. She was sold for scrap in 1920. (*National Maritime Museum N24152*)

HMS *Adventure* (1904). The *Adventure* is in the River Tamar off Devonport Dockyard in 1919. She has been at least partially rearmed, as there are two 4 in guns in shields aft. However, the guns on the forecastle could still be 12 pdrs: there is no sign of AA guns or torpedo tubes. The two Adventures were the last of the original set of eight scout cruisers and became the pattern for future designs. She was sold for scrap in 1920. (*Ian Allan/Science Museum/Science & Society S1148*)

Minotaur Class Armoured Cruisers – three ships, first laid down in January 1905. Legend displacement 14,600 tons; length and beam 519 ft × 74 ft 6 in; power 27,000 ihp for 23 kts; principal armament: four 9.2 in, ten 7.5 in and sixteen 12 pdr guns, five submerged 18 in torpedo tubes; protection: sides, 6 in (max) belt, deck 2 in (max).

HMS *Minotaur* (1906). The *Minotaur* is seen shortly after the funnel bands denoting her place in the 1st Cruiser Squadron were applied in March 1909. She also has range drums on both spotting tops. Unlike the Duke of Edinburgh and Warrior classes, the main armour belt in these ships did not extend above main deck level. There are 12 pdrs on the roofs of the heavy turrets. The prominent useless anti-torpedo nets were removed shortly before war broke out. The preponderance of 7.5s was perhaps a mistake, but the reintroduction of 12 pdrs for anti-flotilla craft defence was a sensible step. (*Ian Allan/Science Museum/Science & Society S1071*)

HMS *Minotaur*. After forming part of the escort for the surrendering German High Seas Fleet on 21 November 1918 the *Minotaur*'s active life was over. Here, she is arriving at Portsmouth on 15 December 1918 to await her ultimate disposal. Compared to the previous plate, she now looks much heavier, with bridgework extended, director-carrying tripod foremast and raised funnels. There are AA guns fore and aft and regrouped searchlights. She was the fastest ship of the class, although only just reaching contract figures, and was sold for scrap in 1920. (*National Maritime Museum N1221*)

HMS *Shannon* (1906). In this 1917 photograph the *Shannon* displays her penultimate form. There are range-finding baffles on the funnels and mainmast, and a 3 in AA gun on aft superstructure. Director control for the heavy guns is not yet fitted. The *Shannon* employed an experimental modified hull form with 1 ft wider beam but shallower draught. This was a failure as, despite exceeding designed power by almost 10 per cent, she failed to reach 22.6 kts. She replaced the *Cochrane* at Murmansk and later visited Archangel before returning to Scotland at the end of November 1918. The whole class originally had short funnels, as directed by Fisher (First Sea Lord), but they were later raised by 15 ft. The *Shannon* was sold for scrap in 1922. (*Royal Naval Museum Portsmouth*)

Boadicea Class   Scout Cruisers – two ships, first laid down in June 1907. Legend displacement 3,300 tons; length and beam 405 ft 9 in × 41 ft; power 18,000 shp for 25 kts; principal armament: six 4 in guns, two 18 in torpedo tubes; protection: 1 in (max) deck (partial).

HMS *Boadicea* (1908). The *Boadicea* is seen minelaying, probably in the North Sea, on 24 February 1918. Protective awnings are rigged aft on the mine deck. Four 4 in guns have been added to the rather weak original armament, plus one 3 in AA. She was unique in having her forward guns on a platform before the bridge. Unlike the earlier scouts, these ships had the great advantage of turbine machinery. The *Boadicea* was sold for scrap in 1926. (*National Maritime Museum N22755*)

Bristol Class   2nd Class Protected Cruisers – five ships, first laid down in February 1909. Legend displacement 4,800 tons; length and beam 453 ft × 4 7ft; power 22,000 shp for 25 kts; principal armament: two 6 in and ten 4 in guns, two submerged 18 in torpedo tubes; protection: 2 in (max) deck.

HMS *Liverpool* (1909). Moving slowly through very calm waters during contractor's trials in 1910, the brand new *Liverpool* has civilians on board, including the bowler-hatted figure right forward. The spray screen to protect the base of the forward 4 in gun mounting is evident. (*VSEL*)

HMS *Liverpool*. In this 1917 Mediterranean scene, the *Liverpool*'s main topmast has been reduced to a stump. A searchlight platform has been added on the foremast, above the bridge, and a 3 in AA gun is on the bandstand between the fourth funnel and the aft rangefinder. Splinter mattresses are fitted at all exposed stations. The *Liverpool* was sold for scrap in 1921. (*Maritime Photo Library 1048*)

HMS *Bristol* (1910). The *Bristol* spent most of the First World War in the Mediterranean and Adriatic, where this image was captured in 1915. The 4 in guns are trained to port and between Nos four and five is the aft control, on which there is a 12 pdr AA gun. As an experiment she was fitted with Brown-Curtis turbines and two-shaft machinery, which produced 24,227 shp for 26.84 kts. On 6 August 1914 she briefly engaged SMS *Karlsruhe*, but unfortunately her speed was temporarily limited to 18 kts by engine trouble, and the German ship outran her. The *Bristol* was sold for scrap in 1921. (*Maritime Photo Library 1044*)

Blonde Class Scout Cruisers – two ships, first laid down in April 1909. Legend displacement 3,350 tons; length and beam 405 ft × 41 ft; power 18,000 shp for 24.5 kts; principal armament: ten 4 in guns, two 21 in torpedo tubes; protection: 1.5 in (max) deck (partial).

HMS *Blonde* (1910). Off Pembroke Dock on 19 May 1911, the *Blonde* has just been completed at the dockyard and handed over to the Royal Navy. An interesting detail is the small cut-out at the forward end either side of the aft deckhouse, to allow the fourth pair of 4 in guns to be trained almost aft. These were the first cruisers to carry 21 in torpedoes, positioned on either beam between the second and third funnels. The *Blonde* was sold for scrap in 1921. (*Public Record Office ADM 176/88*)

Weymouth Class 2nd Class Protected Cruisers – four ships, first laid down November 1909. Legend displacement 5,250 tons; length and beam 453 ft × 48 ft 6 in; power 22,000 shp for 25 kts; principal armament: eight 6 in guns, two submerged 21 in torpedo tubes; protection: 2 in (max) deck.

HMS *Falmouth* (1910). As seen here, the *Falmouth* is in largely original condition pre-war. The tumblehome of the hull section amidships is highlighted by the bulwark above. With their uniform armament of 6 in guns, three of them at forecastle deck level, and 21 in torpedo tubes, these were much more capable ships than the Bristols. (*Ian Allan / Science Museum / Science & Society S316*)

HMS *Falmouth*. At anchor in 1914, just pre-war, with her boarding ladder down, the only notable changes to the *Falmouth*'s appearance are rearranged searchlights. She sank four German merchant ships in August 1914. A tough ship, it took four torpedo hits in four attacks over two days by *U66* and *U52* to sink her in August 1916. (*Maritime Photo Library 1051*)

HMS *Yarmouth* (1911). This photograph shows the *Yarmouth* while serving on the South American Station in September 1920. Late wartime modifications include the installation of a tripod foremast to carry a gunnery director, and a tall searchlight tower aft. She made 26 kts on trials. The *Yarmouth* was sold for scrap in 1929. (*Maritime Photo Library 1053*)

HMS *Weymouth* (1910). Lying at Brindisi in 1918, the *Weymouth* is flying the broad pennant of the Cdre 1st Class commanding 8 LCS. She has been fitted with a main armament director on its supporting tripod, and the platform between the second and third funnels carries a 3 pdr AA gun. On 29 December 1915, with the *Dartmouth* and Italian ships, she was in action off Durazzo against an Austrian force including the light cruiser *Helgoland*, which escaped at 27 kts. The *Weymouth* was sold for scrap in 1928. (*National Maritime Museum 5259*)

Active Class Scout Cruisers – three ships, first laid down in October 1910. Legend displacement 3,440 tons; length and beam 406 ft × 41 ft 6 in; power 18,000 shp for 25 kts; principal armament: ten 4 in guns, two 21 in torpedo tubes; protection: 1 in (max) deck (partial).

HMS *Active* (1911). Seen at high speed sometime in 1917, the *Active* has a 3 in AA gun on the bandstand at the aft end of the forecastle deck. This class, the last of fifteen scout cruisers, differed little from the Blondes, except for the cutaway ram bow in place of the full ram, and double-skinning amidships. The *Active* was sold for scrap in 1920. (*Maritime Photo Library 1123*)

HMS *Fearless* (1912). Leaving Portsmouth in 1919, with Gosport on her starboard side, the *Fearless* reveals several modifications. The most prominent wartime addition is the searchlight platform on the foremast. The layout aft is altered, with rearranged searchlights and aft control. Nos three and four 4 in guns lack shields, while Nos seven and eight appear to have been replaced by two additional torpedo tubes. Because 4 in guns were not given director control, she and similarly-armed cruisers did not receive a tripod foremast. The *Fearless* was sold for scrap in 1921. (*National Maritime Museum N7892*)

Chatham Class 2nd Class Protected Cruisers (belted) – six ships, including three for the Royal Australian Navy, first laid down in January 1911. Legend displacement 5,400 tons; length and beam 458 ft × 49 ft; power 25,000 shp for 25.5 kts; principal armament: eight 6 in guns, two submerged 21 in torpedo tubes; protection: sides, 2 in plating on 1 in hull plating, deck 1.5 in (max).

HMS *Southampton* (1912). Seen off the Northern Isles on a moderate day in the second half of 1915, the *Southampton* has a newly fitted 3 in AA gun aft of the funnels. In 1916 she won fame as Cdre Goodenough's flagship at the Battle of Jutland, being singled out for praise for good cruiser work in keeping the CinC in touch with events. In the night action, at point-blank range, she lost her midships guns and their crews, and was set on fire. However, she sank the light cruiser SMS *Frauenlob*. In this class the forecastle deck was extended well aft, reducing wetness amidships and improving the command of the two waist guns. They were also given a degree of side protection, at the expense of a thinner deck. A further distinguishing feature was the cutaway ram bow. The *Southampton* was sold for scrap in 1926. (*National Maritime Museum N16791*)

HMS *Chatham* (1911). The *Chatham* had been mined off the Norfolk coast on 26 May 1916 and is seen here being towed stern-first into Chatham Dockyard for repairs. The paddle tug is churning up a characteristic wake. Post-war, she was loaned to New Zealand (see Chapter 6, page 162). The *Chatham* was sold for scrap in 1926. (*Maritime Photo Library 1057*)

Birmingham Class Light Cruisers – four ships, including one for the Royal Australian Navy, first laid down in June 1912. Legend displacement 5,440 tons (standard displacement from 1922 5,550 tons); length and beam 457 ft × 50 ft; power 25,000 shp for 25.5 kts; principal armament: nine 6 in guns, two submerged 21 in torpedo tubes; protection: sides, 2 in plating on 1 in hull plating, deck 1.5 in (max).

HMS *Nottingham* (1913). The *Nottingham* is seen here in 1914, perhaps just pre-war. There are awnings rigged extensively aft of the bridge. Although conceived as 2nd class protected cruisers (belted), this class was subsumed into the new light cruiser category before completion. As well as an extra 6 in gun on the forecastle, these ships featured increased flare forward for better seakeeping. The *Nottingham* was torpedoed by *U52* on 19 August 1916. (*Maritime Photo Library 1080*)

HMS *Lowestoft* (1913). The absence of a director on the foretop and of a searchlight tower aft suggests that this photograph of the *Lowestoft* dates from 1915/16. In early 1915 she became the first cruiser to be fitted with a tripod mast. The 3 in AA, fitted in 1915, is between the aft davits. On 2 October 1918 she joined the *Weymouth* and other ships in bombardment of Durazzo. The *Lowestoft* was sold for scrap in 1931. (*Maritime Photo Library 1079*)

HMS *Birmingham* (1913). The scene is Mossel Bay, Cape Province, and the *Birmingham* is preparing for her 1928 East Coast cruise, with the sided 6 in guns on the forecastle deck evident. The Union Castle liner *Arundel Castle* is in the background. On 9 August 1914 she rammed and sank *U15*, the first U-boat to be sunk. She was flagship of 6 LCS on the African Station from 1923 to 1928. The *Birmingham* was sold for scrap in 1931. (*Simon's Town Museum*)

Arethusa Class   Light Cruisers –
eight ships, first laid down in October
1912. Legend displacement 3,512 tons;
length and beam 436 ft × 39 ft; power
40,000 shp for 28.5 kts; principal
armament: two 6 in and six 4 in guns,
four 21 in torpedo tubes; protection:
sides, 2 in on 1 in (partial), deck 1 in
(max) (partial).

HMS *Penelope* (1914). The brand new *Penelope* is
being turned through 90° in Ramsden Dock
Basin at the Barrow yard of Vickers, in order to
proceed out into Walney Channel, in
December 1914. Her 6 pdr AA gun has not yet
been fitted, neither have the splinter
mattresses. On 25 April 1916 she survived
being torpedoed by *UB29* on return from an
unsuccessful chase of a German force which
had bombarded Lowestoft and Yarmouth. The
Arethusas, given extra speed to work with the
latest destroyers, were the first cruisers to rely
exclusively on oil fuel. Although rather
cramped, they were successful ships, from
which a further thirty-eight 6 in light cruisers
of the C, D and E classes evolved. The *Penelope*
was sold for scrap in 1924. (*Cumbria Records
Office*)

HMS *Undaunted* (1914). This scene at Chatham in May 1915 clearly shows the futility of painted-on false bow waves which stop at the boot topping. The *Undaunted* has a 3 in AA gun between the aft pair of 4 in guns, with lighter AA guns (3 or 6 pdr) each side of the centre funnel. The item beyond her bridge, from which the splinter mattresses have been removed, is dockside equipment (see HMS *Calliope*, page 60). On 17 October 1914, in company with three destroyers, the *Undaunted* sank four German destroyers west of Texel. The *Undaunted* was sold for scrap in 1923. (*Public Record Office ADM 176/737*)

The Tondhern Raid, a minor and unsuccessful operation, is under way here on 24 March 1916. The seaplane carrier HMS *Vindex* is being escorted by units of the Harwich force, including the Arethusa class ships: *Aurora* (left), *Undaunted* (right) and *Penelope*; and the Caroline class ships: *Conquest* (centre) and *Cleopatra*, together with leaders and flotilla craft. The *Cleopatra* rammed and sank the German destroyer *G194*, but was then in collision with the *Undaunted*. (*National Maritime Museum N24108*)

HMS *Royalist* (1915). With the *Inconstant* to starboard, the *Royalist* is seen prior to August 1918, when her armament was modified. Earlier that year all the class were fitted with aircraft flying-off platforms over No. one gun: here, Sopwith Camel fighters are on board. Extra pairs of torpedo tubes flank the 4 in AA gun aft, but she retains her heavy armoured conning tower. The *Royalist* was sold for scrap in 1922. (*Fleet Air Arm Museum CARS R/76*)

HMS *Galatea* (1914). Her aircraft flying-off platform is still in place in this 1920 image of the *Galatea*. A third 6 in gun is now mounted ahead of the aft gun. Ahead of this there is an enlarged aft control position, with a rangefinder above two 36 in searchlights, plus two 3 in AA guns. On 4 May 1916, with the *Phaeton*, she shot down Zeppelin *L-7*. Later, at 14.20 on 31 May, she hoisted the signal 'Enemy in sight . . .', thus initiating the Battle of Jutland. The *Galatea* was sold for scrap in 1921. (*Fleet Air Arm Museum CARS G/134*)

Caroline Class Light Cruisers – six ships, first laid down in July 1913. Legend displacement 3,790 tons; length and beam 446 ft × 41 ft 6 in; power 40,000 shp for 28.5 kts; principal armament: two 6 in and eight 4 in guns, two 21 in torpedo tubes; protection: sides, 2 in on 1 in (partial), deck 1 in (max) (partial).

HMS *Caroline* (1914). On a grey and gloomy day in December 1914 the *Caroline* is on builder's trials on the Arran measured mile, making a little over 29 kts. There is a 6 pdr AA gun just ahead of the mainmast. The *Caroline* had been built in the record time of just over ten months. She formed part of 4 LCS at the Battle of Jutland, which engaged German destroyers, sinking the *S35*. The unrestored *Caroline* is still afloat, the second-oldest Royal Navy warship in commission, and is the as-yet uncut jewel in Britain's maritime crown. (*Maritime Photo Library 1133*)

HMS *Cleopatra* (1915). At Devonport Dockyard in about May 1915, the *Cleopatra* is in the final stages of fitting-out under a large sheerlegs. Splinter mattresses are already in place on the bridge, but she is lacking the 6 in guns aft. The sided 4 in guns before the bridge can be clearly seen. This class was an expansion of the Arethusa design, with redistributed armament. (*Public Record Office ADM 176/136*)

HMS *Cleopatra*. Passing Southsea Common inward bound in 1920, the *Cleopatra* shows the principal wartime modifications applied to the class. These included a gunnery director and supporting tripod, and the substitution of two additional 6 in guns for the 4 in LA guns. A pair of 4 in HA guns is mounted abreast the bridge. During the Tondhern raid in March 1916 she rammed and sank the German destroyer *G194*. The *Cleopatra* was sold for scrap in 1931. (*Plymouth Naval Base Museum*)

HMS *Comus* (1914). This private snapshot of the *Comus* was taken while she was on a goodwill visit to Dawlish in Devon during 1929. Like the *Cleopatra*, her main armament now comprises four 6 in guns. She sank the German raider SMS *Greif* on 29 February 1916. The *Comus* was sold for scrap in 1934. (*Simon's Town Museum*)

Calliope Class Light Cruisers – two ships, first laid down in January 1914. Legend displacement 3,835 tons; length and beam 446 ft × 4 1ft 6 in; power 37,500 shp for 28 kts; principal armament: two 6 in and eight 4 in guns, two submerged 21 in torpedo tubes; protection: sides, 2 in on 1 in (partial), deck 1 in (max) (partial).

HMS *Calliope* (1914). Alongside at Chatham in 1915, the *Calliope* wears a vice-admiral's flag at fore as flagship of 4 LCS. She is probably painted in an experimental grey/green shade, and is in original condition, with 4 in guns forward and a 3 pdr AA gun before the mainmast. Fewer but larger boilers permitted one funnel to be suppressed in most light cruisers from this two-ship class onwards. The class also introduced geared turbines, and the torpedo tubes were relocated below the waterline. The *Calliope* was sold for scrap in 1931. (*Public Record Office ADM 176/113*)

HMS *Champion* (1915). Seen here in 1928 while serving as gunnery training ship at Portsmouth, the *Champion* was built with experimental two-shaft machinery which produced 41,188 shp for over 29.5 kts on trials. She shows the standard late-wartime changes, including all-6 in main armament, tripod foremast and revised aft control position. The *Champion* was sold for scrap in 1934. (*Plymouth Naval Base Museum*)

Birkenhead Class

Light Cruisers – two ships, first laid down in April 1914. Legend displacement 5,185 (5,235 Chester) tons; length and beam 446 ft (456 ft 6 in Chester) × 50 ft; power 25,000 shp for 25.5 kts (31,000/26.5 Chester); principal armament: ten 5.5 in and two 3 in guns, two submerged 21 in torpedo tubes; protection: sides, 2 in on 1 in, deck 1.5 in (max).

HMS *Birkenhead* (1915). Fitting-out at the Cammell Laird shipyard on 20 January 1915, the *Birkenhead* had been launched just two days earlier. All the major superstructure items are in place, but only one gun has been installed. The sided AA gun bandstands forward of the aft 5.5 in gun are a noteworthy feature at this early date. Both she and the *Chester* had originally been ordered by Greece. (*Cammell Laird Archives/Wirral Museum*)

HMS *Birkenhead*. The ship is now complete and is seen in the River Mersey. The efficient new Coventry Ordnance Works 5.5 in guns are clearly seen. These were excellent anti-destroyer weapons, having a higher rate of fire than the usual 6 in. The same type of gun was used in the *Hood* and *Furious*. At this date the foremast is not yet a tripod, despite appearances. The bridge has the usual protection. The *Birkenhead* was sold for scrap in 1921. (*Cammell Laird Archives/Wirral Museum*)

HMS *Chester* (1915). Also proceeding along the Mersey is the *Chester*, a better-looking ship than the *Birkenhead*. She was 10 ft longer and her mainmast, much further aft, matched the rake of the foremast. Unlike the *Birkenhead*, the *Chester* burnt oil fuel only. At the Battle of Jutland she was in action against RAd Boediker's light cruisers, SMS *Frankfurt*, *Elbing*, *Pilau* and *Wiesbaden*. She was smothered with bursting shells and within five minutes three guns on the engaged side were disabled. Boy Cornwall won his posthumous VC in this action. The *Chester* was sold for scrap in 1921. (*Cammell Laird Archives/Wirral Museum*)

Cambrian Class Light Cruisers – four ships, first laid down in October 1914. Legend displacement 3,825 tons; length and beam 446 ft × 41 ft 6 in; power 40,000 shp for 29 kts; principal armament: two 6 in and eight 4 in guns (*Cambrian* three 6 in and six 4 in), two submerged 21 in torpedo tubes; protection: sides, 2 in on 1 in (partial), deck 1 in (max) (partial).

HMS *Castor* (1915). Running contractor's speed trials in about November 1915, and revealing its very businesslike profile, the *Castor* is making commendably little smoke. There is a 3 pdr AA gun ahead of the stump mainmast. This class reverted to direct-drive turbines. The *Castor* was sold for scrap in 1936. (*Cammell Laird Archives / Wirral Museum*)

HMS *Canterbury* (1915). Completing in April or very early May 1916, the *Canterbury* is being eased out of the John Brown shipyard on the Clyde. The two 6 in guns have not yet been fitted aft. In these ships, which were basically two-funnelled Carolines, the top outer edge of 4 in gun shields is not cut back. The *Canterbury* was sold for scrap in 1934. (*Business Records Centre, University of Glasgow*)

HMS *Cambrian* (1916). The ship seen here at high speed in this rather distant early 1918 snapshot is most probably the *Cambrian*, although there remains a slight possibility that it could be the *Constance*. The *Cambrian* was fitted with an additional 6 in gun in place of the paired 4 in on the forecastle of her sisters before she joined the fleet. Post-Jutland modifications included a tripod mast and director, while the aircraft flying-off platform before the bridge had been fitted during the winter of 1917/18. There appear to be deck-mounted torpedo tubes aft. The *Cambrian* was sold for scrap in 1934. (*Plymouth Naval Base Museum*)

Centaur Class Light Cruisers – two ships, first laid down in January 1915. Legend displacement 3,825 tons; length and beam 446 ft × 42 ft; power 40,000 shp for 29 kts; principal armament: five 6 in and two 3 in guns, two submerged 21 in torpedo tubes; protection: sides, 2 in on 1 in (partial), deck 1 in (max) (partial).

HMS *Concord* (1916). Although of poor quality, the rarity of this photograph of a cruiser of one of the 'C' classes painted in dazzle justifies its inclusion. The *Concord* is operating a kite balloon while serving with the Harwich Force in September 1917. Both ships of this class were built to utilize materials assembled for two cancelled ships for Turkey. The *Concord* was sold for scrap in 1935. (*National Maritime Museum N22756*)

HMS *Centaur* (1916). This image dates from early 1918, and shows the *Centaur*'s modified aft control. A strong AA armament is now carried: two 3 in, one before and one aft of aft control position, and two pom-poms aft of No. four 6 in gun. The two ships of the Centaur class were the first to be built with a uniform centreline armament of 6 in guns. For this, an extra gun had been worked in immediately aft of the foremast, necessitating moving the bridge forward some 28 ft. The resulting profile is not elegant. The *Centaur* was sold for scrap in 1934. (*National Maritime Museum N11689*)

Hawkins Class Light Cruisers – five ships, first laid down in December 1915. Legend displacement 9,750 tons (standard displacement from 1922 9,879 [av]); length and beam 605 ft × 65 ft; power 60,000–70,000 shp for 30–31 kts; principal armament: seven 7.5 in and ten 3 in (*Hawkins* and *Raleigh*)/three 4 in guns (*Effingham* and *Frobisher*), six 21 in torpedo tubes; protection: sides, 2 in on 1 in (max), deck 1.5 in (max) (partial). The *Vindictive* completed as a carrier with reduced armament.

HMS *Hawkins* (1917). With the old *Shannon* in the background, awaiting her fate, the new *Hawkins* is completing alongside at Chatham in mid-1919. She is painted in China Station colours of white hull and light grey upperworks, to become flagship of the First World War hero VAd Tyrwhitt. The secondary armament, a mixture of low- and high-angle 3 in (12 pdr) guns, includes two firing through lidded ports in the forward superstructure just visible below No. two 7.5 in gun's blast deflector. The ships of this class were the first cruisers to exceed 600 ft and 30 kts. They were developed from the Birmingham class via the abortive Atlantic cruisers of 1912/13. The foreground of the original photograph has been subjected to censoring. (*Public Record Office ADM 176/323*)

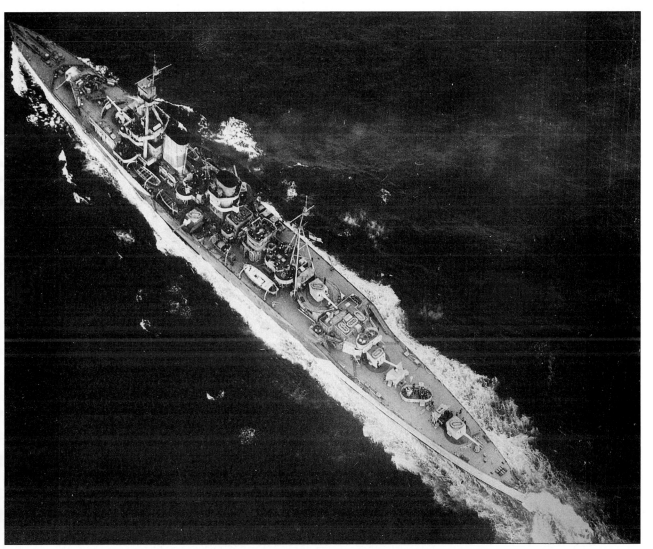

HMS *Hawkins*. When this overhead view was taken in late 1942, the *Hawkins'* subsidiary armament comprised four single 4 in, two quad and two single pom-poms (the latter prominent on the quarterdeck between Nos six and seven 7.5 in guns) and seven single 20 mm Oerlikon automatic AA cannon, coupled with the standard radar outfit. The aerials of the Type 281 air warning radar appear blurred because they are revolving in the search mode. Her single destroyer-type rangefinder director Mk IV is between the second funnel and the mainmast. When new she had mixed oil and coal-fired 60,000 shp machinery for 30 kts, but her four coal-fired boilers were removed in 1929 and replaced by extra oil tanks. However, the *Hawkins* could still make 29.5 kts with 55,000 shp. She was sold for scrap in 1947. (*Royal Navy*)

HMS *Raleigh* (1919). The *Raleigh*, seen completing at Beardmore's Glasgow yard in 1919, was the only member of the class to receive 70,000 shp machinery, with which she made 31 kts on trials in September 1920. The port for the 12 pdr gun under No. two 7.5 in has its covers clipped over it. The best of the class, she unfortunately ran aground in bad weather on Point Amour on the Labrador side of the Strait of Belle Isle on 8 August 1922 and became a total loss. In this class there was 1–2 in high-tensile steel protective plating applied over the whole length of the hull, much of which was itself plated with 1 in HT steel. The staggered edge of the 1 in upper plating forward can be seen. (*Maritime Photo Library 1236*)

HMS *Vindictive* (1918). During her varied career the *Vindictive* served as an aircraft carrier, cruiser, training cruiser and repair ship. She is seen here in 1937/38 in the training rôle, with the aft funnel (and the boilers it served) removed and substantial deck-houses added to accommodate up to 200 cadets. Her only weapons are two single 4.7 in guns forward, with the short shields which led to so many leg injuries in wartime. From her days as a carrier she retains the aircraft hangar and handling crane before the bridge: there is another crane aft. The items on the hangar side are compressed air cylinders which served the aircraft catapult formerly carried. Ordered as the *Cavendish*, she was renamed in June 1918 to commemorate the heroine of the Zeebrugge Raid. The *Vindictive* was sold for scrap in 1946. (*Courtesy* The News, *Portsmouth*)

HMS *Effingham* (1921). The *Effingham* was the second ship of this class to be wrecked, as seen here on 18 May 1940. While transporting troops and supplies to Bødø during the Norwegian Campaign, she ran aground on a 2 fathom patch and settled by the head, with all engine and boiler rooms flooded. The proximity of enemy forces made salvage impossible and the ship was sunk by Royal Navy ships on 21 May: there were no casualties. Inevitably, the Germans photographed the abandoned wreck lying on its starboard side, claiming that it had been sunk by the Luftwaffe. When reconstructed in 1937/38 she had been given nine obsolete single 6 in guns taken from AA conversions of the C classes: a waste of a good hull. She also received four twin 4 in, controlled by two HADT MkIII, two octuple pom-poms and three quad 0.5 in heavy machine-guns, but no radar. A catapult was fitted and a *Walrus* aircraft operated in Norwegian waters. Boilers were reduced and the uptakes retrunked into one large funnel to give only 58,000 shp for 29.75 kts, but additional fuel was carried, as with the *Hawkins*. (*Fleet Air Arm Museum CARS E/80*)

HMS *Frobisher* (1920). Photographed on 19 February 1944, freshly repainted, the *Frobisher* now has single 20 mm guns atop the armoured shields to Nos two and four 7.5 in guns. Deactivated pre-war, she was rearmed in 1942 with five of her original seven 7.5 in guns. Her AA armament comprised five single 4 in, controlled by two rangefinder directors MkIV in lieu of HADT, and seven 20 mm guns. She also received four quad pom-poms, giving her the most effective close-range armament of any British cruiser at that time. The standard radar outfit includes Type 285 on the RD MkIVs. Her engines produced 65,000 shp for 30.5 kts. The three ships which served as cruisers in the Second World War retained their original First World War-vintage main armament directors. (*Fleet Air Arm Museum CARS F/181*)

HMS *Frobisher*. After being modified to serve as a training cruiser the *Frobisher* is seen on the Clyde on 1 May 1945. Nos two and five 7.5 in guns have been replaced by a 6 in gun and a modern quadruple torpedo tube mounting respectively. Her AA armament is confined to one of the original 4 in, retained on the quarterdeck, and thirteen single 20 mm guns. The starboard RD, together with its supporting tower, has been removed, as has the masthead Type 281 radar. However, she has gained IFF Type 242M at the head of the foremast. The *Frobisher* was sold for scrap in 1949. (*Royal Navy*)

Caledon Class Light Cruisers – four ships, first laid down in February 1916. Legend displacement 4,120 tons (standard displacement from 1922 4,180); length and beam 45 ft × 42 ft 9 in; power 40,000 shp for 29.25 kts; principal armament: five 6 in and two 3 in guns, eight 21 in torpedo tubes; protection: sides, 2 in on 1 in (partial), deck 1 in (max) (partial).

HMS *Caledon* (1916). Anchored in the Mersey after completion in March 1917, the *Caledon* has 3 in AA guns abreast the forward funnel and the usual splinter mattresses protect the upper and lower bridge. Except for the raked bow and geared two-shaft machinery, this class was broadly similar to the Centaurs. They had a heavier torpedo armament than contemporary destroyers, the two port sets of tubes being clearly seen. (*Cammell Laird Archives/Wirral Museum*)

HMS *Caledon*. In April 1945, her active life over, the *Caledon* is being towed to a reserve berth, stripped of all armament. Converted to an AA cruiser in 1942/43, she was the last and oldest of the C classes to be so modified, and looks nothing like her original self. For her new rôle she had to be rebuilt forward of the funnels on the lines of the Ceres class to accommodate a comprehensive and modern AA armament. This was the oldest class to see service in both world wars. The *Caledon* was sold for scrap in 1948. (*Maritime Photo Library 1153*)

HMS *Cassandra* (1916). The date is 29 June 1917, and the *Cassandra* is seen on the Skelmorlie measured mile during contractor's full power sea trials, when a speed of 29.1 kts was reached. She displays an interesting two-tone paint scheme. There is a small aircraft hangar next to the bridge for experiments in launching a fighter from ramps on the forecastle deck. For these, the first production Beardmore WBIII S.B.3F (N6100) was employed. The *Cassandra* was lost on an uncharted German minefield off the island of Oesel (Hiiumaa) in the Baltic, on 5 December 1918, while operating against the Bolsheviks. (*VSEL*)

HMS *Calypso* (1917). Although it is July 1935 it could be ten years earlier, as the old small cruisers had ceased to be worth modernizing in their intended rôle as fleet vessels. With the copious bunting she makes a colourful sight. Compared to the two earlier ships of this class, the most visible change is the reduction and resiting of 36 in searchlights. There are now only two, on the aft control with the HA rangefinder. The *Calypso* was torpedoed by the Italian submarine *Alpino Bagnolini* on 12 June 1940. (*Maritime Photo Library 1156*)

Ceres Class   Light Cruisers – five ships, first laid down in July 1916. Legend displacement 4,190 tons (standard 4,290); length and beam 450 ft × 43 ft 6 in; power 40,000 shp for 29 kts; principal armament: five 6 in and two 3 in guns, eight 21 in torpedo tubes; protection: sides, 2 in on 1 in (partial), deck 1 in (max) (partial).

HMS *Ceres* (1917). The first of the new class to complete, the *Ceres* is seen leaving the John Brown shipyard in June 1917. This handsome class was a milestone design, with No. two 6 in gun in a superfiring position above No. one. To accommodate this, the boiler rooms were moved aft by 18 ft and the bridge and foremast by 46 ft. Beam was increased by 9 in. When new they were the finest light cruisers in the world. They saw service late in the First World War and were worked hard in the Second World War. The *Ceres* was sold for scrap in 1946. (*Public Record Office ADM 176/896*)

HMS *Cardiff* (1917). In this historic photograph the *Cardiff* has the honour of leading in the German High Seas Fleet to surrender on 21 November 1918. At the head of the German line of seventy warships is the almost indestructible battlecruiser SMS *Seydlitz*. The *Cardiff* is flying a kite balloon, and there is a non-rigid airship on the left . (*Public Record Office ADM 176/887*)

HMS *Cardiff*. Here, the *Cardiff* is seen in the Clyde in 1944, towards the end of her third conflict (she had operated against the Bolsheviks in 1918/19). RMS *Queen Elizabeth* is in the background. Serving as a gunnery training ship during most of the Second World War, she has received little modern equipment, just six single 20 mm guns and radar Types 290 (at head of foremast) and 273. The camouflage is Admiralty Emergency Light or Intermediate Type (depending on interpretation of shades). The *Cardiff* was sold for scrap in 1946. (*National Maritime Museum N31441*)

HMS *Curlew* (1917). This photograph was taken at Esquimalt, British Columbia, on 17 November 1929. Many cruisers spent the inter-war years Showing the Flag in distant ports. A range clock is mounted before the gunnery director. In August 1939 the *Curlew*, by then converted to an AA cruiser, was fitted with radar Type 79Z, some five times more powerful than the fleet's prototype set fitted earlier to the *Sheffield*. The *Curlew* was bombed on 26 May 1940. (*Simon's Town Museum*)

HMS *Coventry* (1917). The *Coventry* reveals her (for the time) formidable AA armament when seen here on 15 January 1936, after she and the *Curlew* had been converted as the prototype AA cruisers. All original weapons and directors have been removed and replaced by ten single 4 in HA and two octuple pom-poms. Two HADT and platforms for pom-pom directors have been added, but the directors themselves are awaited. The empty aft PD platform is between the aft HADT and No. eight gun. Such conversions gave a boost to the fleet's weak AA defence and offered a new lease of life to otherwise-obsolete ships. (*Public Record Office ADM 176/164*)

HMS *Coventry*. Numerous minor changes are evident in this photograph, taken off Alexandria on 12 May 1941. Owing to a shortage of mountings the aft octuple pom-pom has been replaced by two quad 0.5 in. Also, Nos six and seven 4 in have been landed. There is a new fore topmast, with the fore HADT moved forward and raised, and a tripod mainmast. The forward pom-pom director is in place and there are aerials for Type 279 radar at the mastheads. The *Coventry* was bombed on 14 September 1942. (*National Maritime Museum N31487*)

HMS *Curacoa* (1917). The *Curacoa* is at anchor at Scapa Flow, possibly after being damaged by aircraft at Andalsnes on 24 April 1940. The receiver for Type 279 radar at the head of the mainmast appears to be damaged, perhaps by whiplash. In her conversion to an AA cruiser, four twin 4 in have replaced all 6 in guns, there is a quad pom-pom before the bridge, and two quad 0.5 in are abreast the forward funnel. A useless UP launcher is in a zareba between the aft 4 in mountings. The *Curacoa* was lost in collision on 2 October 1942. (*National Maritime Museum N31500*)

Danae Class   Light Cruisers – three ships, first laid down in December 1916. Legend displacement 4,765 tons (standard 4,835); length and beam 471 ft × 46 ft; power 40,000 shp for 29 kts; principal armament: six 6 in and two 3 in guns, twelve 21 in torpedo tubes; protection: sides, 2 in on 1 in (partial), deck 1 in (max) (partial).

HMS *Dragon* (1917). In this tranquil inter-war picture, dating from about 1931, the *Dragon* is possibly off the coast of Canada. She has been modified to carry three 4 in AA, two abreast fore funnel and one aft of No. five 6 in gun, and single pom-poms in the bridge wings. There is a range clock facing aft at the base of the mainmast. In this class an additional 6 in gun was worked in aft of the funnels, while the heavy torpedo armament was outstanding. She was later loaned to Poland (*Ian Allan/Science Museum/Science & Society S585*)

HMS *Dauntless* (1918). The *Dauntless* is a sad sight after running aground off Cap Thrum, Nova Scotia, on 2 July 1928. She has had much top hamper, including guns and funnels, removed to lighten her so that she can be refloated and towed off, badly damaged, on 12 July. Repaired, she remained active through most of the Second World War. The *Dauntless* was sold for scrap in 1946. (*J.C.M. Hayward/National Archives of Canada PA-164892*)

HM Ships *Danae* (1918), *Arethusa* and *Frobisher*, plus ORP *Dragon*, part of Force D (RAd Patterson), are moving into position on 5 June 1944 to provide fire support for the D-Day landings next day at 'Sword' beach, near Lyon-sur-Mer. The *Arethusa's* second funnel had been shortened by this date. The *Frobisher* and *Dragon* fell victim to underwater attack on 8 July and 8 August respectively. The heavy cruiser survived to serve post-war, but the light cruiser did not (see Poland in Chapter 6, p. 172). The *Danae* was later loaned to Poland to replace the *Dragon*. (*Public Record Office ADM 199/1662*)

Carlisle Class Light Cruisers – five ships, first laid down in October 1917. Legend displacement 4,290 tons (standard 4,200); length and beam 451 ft 6in × 43 ft 6 in; power 40,000 shp for 29.5 kts; principal armament: five 6 in and two 3 in guns, eight 21 in torpedo tubes; protection: sides, 2 in on 1 in (partial), deck 1 in (max) (partial).

HMS *Capetown* (1919). It is 28 June 1919 and launch day for the *Capetown*, which is already entering the water. Clearly visible is the angle or knuckle formed where the new raised forecastle deck rises vertically from the original hull line. This raised deck was dubbed a trawler bow, and was introduced to reduce the wetness forward that plagued the earlier Cs and Danaes. Rather than completely redesign the whole of the forward hull, a revised deckline simply swept up to the stem from No. one gun. Because of this the anchors were moved above the knuckle. This innovation, considered so successful that it featured on all but one future British cruiser, was not adopted abroad. (*Cammell Laird Archives / Wirral Museum*)

HMS *Capetown*. Very little is known about this rare photograph of the *Capetown*, in which she is wearing early camouflage similar to that of the *Ajax* (see p. 96). The date is likely to be prior to April 1941, when she was torpedoed by an Italian MAS, as she would most likely have been repainted after major repairs. She was the only ship in her class not to have been converted to an AA cruiser, and was sold for scrap in 1946. (*Plymouth Naval Base Museum*)

HMS *Carlisle* (1918). After a refit which provided five twin 20 mm and an enhanced radar outfit, the *Carlisle* is at anchor off Plymouth in November 1942. The radar suite now includes Type 281 at the mastheads, surmounted forward by the Type 241 IFF, Type 285 on the HADT and Type 282 on the pom-pom director on the bridge. The Type 271 lantern is 'wooded' by the mainmast. She had been converted to an AA ship at Chatham in 1939/40, losing all her 6 in guns and other armament and receiving instead four twin 4 in HA, a quadruple pom-pom between the forward 4 in and the bridge, and a variety of lighter AA guns. She had also at that time received Type 280, the prototype of Type 281. The *Carlisle* was bombed on 9 October 1943, but although a constructive total loss she was not sold for scrap until 1949. (*Plymouth Naval Base Museum*)

HMS *Colombo* (1918). The *Colombo* is riding off Plymouth in June 1943, after conversion to an AA cruiser at Devonport. All early armament has been removed and replaced by three twin 4 in HA mountings, two twin Bofors in stabilized Hazemeyer mountings (starboard mounting visible just forward of the tripod leg of the mainmast), plus six twin and two single 20 mm, marking a shift of emphasis away from long-range towards close-range AA fire. The radar outfit includes the newer Type 279B at the mainmast head. The *Colombo* was sold for scrap in 1948. (*Plymouth Naval Base Museum*)

Delhi Class Light Cruisers – five ships, first laid down in October 1917. Legend displacement 4,765 tons (4,850 standard); length and beam 472 ft 6 in × 46 ft 6 in; power 40,000 shp for 29 kts; principal armament: six 6 in and two 3 in guns, twelve 21 in torpedo tubes; protection: sides, 2 in on 1 in (partial), deck 1 in (max) (partial).

HMS *Dunedin* (1918). This photograph was taken from one of HMS *Eagle*'s Swordfish during Operation Salvage. With the *Eagle*, the *Dunedin* intercepted the Kriegsmarine supply tanker *Lothringen* (10,746 grt) in mid-Atlantic on 15 June 1941. This was formerly the Dutch *Papendrecht* and was taken into service as the *Empire Salvage*. The interesting camouflage scheme on the *Dunedin* has a shortening effect. Among earlier captures, the *Dunedin* had taken the new German cargo-liner *Hannover*, which became famous after conversion to the first escort carrier, HMS *Audacity*. She is little-modified, except for the provision of Type 286 radar and the substitution of two quad 0.5 in for her two original single pom-poms. The five ships of this class were trawler-bowed versions of the earlier Danaes, as the Capetowns were to the Ceres class. The *Dunedin* was torpedoed by *U124* on 24 November 1941. (*Public Record Office ADM 199/809*)

HMS *Delhi* (1918). The date is 31 March 1942 and the *Delhi* has just emerged from Devonport after receiving radar Types 271, 281, 282 and 285. The buoys of an anti-torpedo net are close astern. During late 1941 she had been refitted in the USA, and given an armament little different to that of contemporary US destroyers of less than half her tonnage: five single US pattern 5 in DP guns controlled by a pair of excellent US Mk37 directors. Close-range armament comprises two quad pom-poms with radar-controlled directors abreast the fore funnel, and eight single hand-operated Oerlikons. The *Delhi* was not fully repaired after damage on 12 February 1945 and was sold for scrap in 1948. (*Plymouth Naval Base Museum*)

HMS *Diomede* (1919). Off Rosyth in June 1943, the *Diomede* has just completed a refit to convert her for service as a training cruiser. The original weatherproof gun house forward (see New Zealand in Chapter 6, p. 163) has been replaced by a standard 6 in gun shield, and No. two gun has in turn received a blast deflector. There are three single 4 in HA, two of them fitted as original equipment. Also, she has two twin and six single 20 mm. Almost invisible at the head of the mainmast is the aerial for Type 290 radar. The stepped-down edge of the armour belt, which stops at the aft 6 in gun, can be clearly seen. The *Diomede* was sold for scrap in 1946. (*National Maritime Museum*)

Emerald Class Light Cruisers – two ships, first laid down in June 1918. Standard displacement 7,565 tons (av); length and beam 570 ft × 54 ft 6 in; power 80,000 shp for 33 kts; principal armament: seven 6 in and three 4 in guns, twelve 21 in torpedo tubes; protection: sides, 2 in on 1 in, deck 1 in (max) (partial).

HMS *Enterprise* (1919). This interesting photograph dates from between mid-May and July 1942, when the *Illustrious* and *Indomitable* in the background were in self-maintenance at Mombassa after taking part in the occupation of Diego Suarez. It not only reveals an interesting camouflage scheme, but shows that the *Enterprise* had received no additional close-range weapons (in the part of the ship visible) or radar by then. Also, the tripod foremast has been shortened and there appear to be no torpedo tubes. A 700 Squadron Fairey Seafox, coded '9Y', is on the catapult. The *Enterprise* was the first warship to complete with a director control tower for the main armament, the prototype of what became a standard fitment. Just before the mainmast is her HADT MkI. (*Fleet Air Arm Museum CARS E/296*)

HMS *Enterprise*. In this November 1943 view we see a much more up-to-date *Enterprise*. Except that it lacks any single 20 mm guns, her close-range armament mirrors that of the *Emerald* (see next plate), and her radar includes Type 284 on the DCT. A new foremast has been fitted and the prototype twin 6 in turret is just visible forward. There appear to be spare torpedoes stowed on deck abreast the catapult, which carries a special Kingfisher-type trolley. With the *Glasgow* she sank the German destroyer *Z27* and fleet torpedo boats *T25* and *26* in bad weather on 28 December 1943. The *Enterprise* was sold for scrap in 1946. (*Royal Navy*)

HMS *Emerald* (1920). The date is 26 May 1944, some seven weeks after completion of the *Emerald*'s final refit. During this her catapult had been removed, and there are now two single 20 mm and two Carley floats on the former base. Of the other four additional singles, two are on the forecastle deck just forward of the stacked Carley floats abreast the second funnel. The others may be at the same level abreast the tripod legs of the foremast. In addition to the original principal armament, she also has two quad pom-poms and six twin 20 mm. Her sensors do not include Type 284 gunnery radar. Fire control equipment is limited to her original director and one MkI HADT. These two ships were expanded Ds, greatly lengthened and with double the power for an additional 4 kts. The *Emerald* was sold for scrap in 1948. (*Royal Navy*)

4 INTERNATIONAL TREATIES AND A BRIEF PEACE

The end of the First World War left nations with massive debts and there was a general belief in the fallacy that disarmament would bring peace (or at least that is what people wanted to believe). International disarmament treaties were seen as the way ahead. The first to affect navies was the Washington Naval Treaty of 1922. This limited the size of both navies and of ships, and had far-reaching consequences, touching many of the vessels which served in the Second World War. As far as cruisers were concerned, the major effect was to impose maximum limits of 10,000 tons and 8 in guns. These limits might have been lower, but the British wished to retain the new Hawkins class cruisers, some of which had not yet completed, while the Americans wished to retain the 8 in gun for their big cruisers. The British and others decided to build up to the new limits, but the impossibility of providing adequate speed, endurance, protection, armament, seakeeping, habitability, etc., on 10,000 tons was soon realized. The thirteen ships in the three classes of the County group, the natural successors to the Hawkins class, were the Royal Navy's compromise response. These lofty vessels, often criticized and derided, proved to be tough ships and served with distinction across the world throughout the Second World War. A change of government saw the original order cut back, but the situation was helped by an order for two from Australia. From about the time of the introduction of these vessels, British cruisers of all types officially became simply cruisers, the term 'light' being dropped in theory.

The main effects of the London Naval Treaty of 1930 were to divide cruisers into two types – those with guns above 6.1 in (155 mm) calibre and those with guns not above that size, and to limit the number of ships in each of the two categories which each signatory might have. The two categories became generally referred to as heavy and light cruisers. Its existing tonnage led the British Commonwealth to be restricted to building ships in the lower category to a total of 91,000 tons, allowing thirteen 6 in ships of the Leander type, which suited the Royal Navy well enough.

Kent Class Heavy Cruisers – seven ships, including two for the Royal Australian Navy, first laid down in September 1924. Standard displacement 9,803 tons (av); length and beam 630 ft × 68 ft 5 in; power 80,000 shp for 31.5 kts; principal armament: eight 8 in and four 4 in guns, eight 21 in torpedo tubes; protection sides, 1 in (partial), deck 1.5 in (max) (partial).

HMS *Kent* (1926). Seen leaving Portsmouth, probably on 27 August 1931, the *Kent* wears the standard China Station paint scheme of white hull and light grey upperworks. A Fairey Flycatcher sits on the catapult. The first so-called Treaty cruiser built up to the 10,000 ton, 8 in gun limit set by the Washington Treaty, the Kents were dignified and imposing ships. They were fitted with the latest fire control: a forward director tower (FDT) with, and an aft director tower (ADT) without, a rangefinder, plus a MkI HADT aft. Designed with short funnels, these were soon raised by 15 ft in the Royal Navy ships because of smoke problems. Virtually unarmoured as built, some protection from underwater attack was afforded by external bulges, hidden here by the boot topping. Apart from their poor protection they were natural descendants of the Hawkins class. (*Plymouth Naval Base Museum*)

Another result was that the earlier Hawkins class, whose protection made them light cruisers when built, moved into the higher category by virtue of their 7.5 in (190 mm) guns.

The five Leanders, with four twin 6 in turrets, were followed by the three Amphions and four Arethusas, which were four- and three-turret developments with divided machinery spaces for better damage control. The Amphions were in turn followed by ten Towns, the first eight of which were basically triple-turret developments of these. These ten large ships, built in response to American and Japanese ships with five triple turrets, were not only the first British cruisers with such turrets, but also introduced built-in aircraft hangars.

From the mid-1930s, ships of this period which had been completed with single 4 in guns gradually had these replaced by twin mountings. Although the *Exeter* and *Sussex* showed what could be done, even after modernization most 8 in cruisers had their mainmasts right aft, where they 'wooded' directors and radar. HMS *London* was completely rebuilt above deck during a partial and not completely successful modernization.

HMS *Kent*. Wearing a four-colour camouflage scheme, the *Kent* is seen after her late-1942 refit. Aircraft arrangements have gone and she has Type 273 radar ahead of the mainmast. Type 241 IFF is above the Type 281 transmitting array on the foremast. Basic fire control is also updated, with the FDT replaced by a late-pattern 8 in director control tower, the former having been moved aft to replace the less capable ADT. There is now an HADT each side of the bridge. A shallow waterline belt of 4.5 in armour has been added to the whole class. Close-range armament includes two octuple pom-poms and eight single 20 mm. The alternate bands of colour are believed to be light grey, pale blue, dark grey and medium blue, although the rear lighting in this view renders the changes of shade aft of the bridge almost invisible. The *Kent* was sold for scrap in 1948. (*Portsmouth Royal Dockyard Historical Trust*)

Between the wars there was little for the Royal Navy's cruisers to do except exercises and Showing the Flag worldwide. One new priority was training ships' AA gun crews, but this was largely unrealistic, as the targets' speed was barely 100 mph and they usually travelled parallel to the firing ship. The fact that, nevertheless, few were hit seems to have provoked little concern.

Towards the end of this period the Abyssinian Crisis prompted the temporary reinforcement of the Mediterranean Fleet, in the fruitless hope of dissuading Mussolini from aggression. Then, the Spanish Civil War necessitated the introduction of non-intervention and neutrality patrols to protect British interests. By then war clouds were again gathering.

HMS *Suffolk* (1926). Bombed by Ju 88s off Stavanger on 17 April 1940, after bombarding the airfield, the *Suffolk* managed to reach Scapa Flow next day in this condition, with her bows up and quarterdeck (which had been cut down like the *Cumberland*'s (see p. 89) under water. She is wearing camouflage on her upperworks only, the colours appearing to be small patches of white and light grey on the standard dark grey base colour – also worn by the *Norfolk* at this time. Her AA armament now comprises four twin 4 in, two quad pom-poms and two quad 0.5 in. She has an external degaussing coil and Type 279 radar. Later, equipped with Type 284 radar, she played a vital rôle in the Bismarck operation, and was sold for scrap in 1948. (*Simon's Town Museum*)

HMS *Berwick* (1926). It is July 1945, and the European war is over. Here, the *Berwick* lies alongside a Bellona class cruiser at Portsmouth, ready for her first Far East trooping trip. Although the radar suite has been updated to include Type 281B, which the newer ship lacks, the close-range AA outfit is unimpressive, because her octuple pom-poms have been replaced by two quads, and there are but five twin and four single Oerlikons. She is painted in the Late Standard Scheme (light grey with medium blue panel), and the 8 in and 4 in turrets are white for aircraft recognition (see also the *Devonshire*, p. 91). The *Berwick* was sold for scrap in 1948. (*Maritime Photo Library 1243*)

HMS *Cumberland* (1926). Still unmistakably a County, but with modern lattice masts of greater load-bearing capacity, the *Cumberland* is seen in about 1950 in her post-war guise as a trials ship. A wide variety of weapons were installed at various times, including the new automatic turrets for the modified Tiger class cruisers, but here she has a single 4.5 in gun, as used in the later Type 81 (Tribal class) frigates, on A barbette. There is a torpedo tube at the extreme stern and what looks like a large rangefinder on Y barbette. The modern radar suite includes Types 277Q, 293Q and 960. Also, there is a YE-60 aircraft homing beacon ahead of the mainmast. Whip aerials, associated with post-war communications systems, are on each funnel. The *Cumberland* was sold for scrap in 1959. (*Portsmouth Royal Dockyard Historical Trust*)

London Class Heavy Cruisers – four ships, first laid down in February 1926. Standard displacement 9,840 tons (av); length and beam 632 ft 8 in × 66 ft; power 80,000 shp for 32.25 kts; principal armament: eight 8 in and four 4 in guns, eight 21 in torpedo tubes; protection: sides, 1in (partial), deck 1.5 in (max) (partial).

HMS *London* (1927). A new ship, the *London* is seen shortly after completion in 1929, as the absent catapult was fitted during a 1930/31 refit. Four single pom-poms are on platforms between the first and second funnels. As there were no external anti-torpedo bulges, beam was reduced and maximum speed increased. Compared to the Kents the layout of the Londons and Dorsetshires was significantly altered, giving a less pleasing profile. The bridge was moved 15 ft aft, with the first and second funnels moved back towards the third, which retained its original position. Increased rake at the bow moved the stem 32 in forward, while both X and Y turrets were moved 5 ft aft. (*Ian Allan/Science Museum/Science & Society S378*)

HMS *London*. Arriving at Malta in early 1946, the *London* is in wartime condition after service with the East Indies Fleet. By this time her close-range armament comprised two octuple pom-poms, four single Bofors plus eight twin and four single 20 mm. Her radar suite still includes Type 279, barely distinguishable against the bright sky, but she now has Type 277, poorly sited before the mainmast. She was the only ship of the County classes to have been reconstructed (after which she bore a passing resemblance to the Fiji class), and when she emerged in February 1941 she had received a 3.5 in armour belt, raising her standard displacement to 11,015 tons. The *London* was sold for scrap in 1950. (*Maritime Photo Library 1272*)

HMS *Sussex* (1928). Reminiscent of the *Suffolk* (see p. 88), this photograph of the *Sussex* shows her after being bombed while unattended during refit in York Hill Basin at Fairfield's Govan shipyard on 18 September 1940. She is listing 23° to starboard with her bows afloat and stern aground. Bomb damage, fire and fire-fighting contributed to disastrous flooding: her repairs taking two years. Noteworthy features include the many sealed scuttles, external degaussing coil and the UP launcher on X turret. The *Sussex* was sold for scrap in 1950. (*Public Record Office ADM 267/81*)

HMS *Devonshire* (1927). Photographed from a Coastal Command aircraft on 13 May 1945, the *Devonshire* is carrying Prince Olaf on his return to Norway. A Norwegian flag is flying with the White Ensign from the mainmast. To aid recognition from the air all turrets are white, as is the DCT, contrasting with the very dark decks. She has lost X turret to compensate for the weight of an enhanced close-range battery comprising six quad pom-poms, plus seventeen twin and six single 20 mm. She sank the German AMC *Atlantis* on 22 November 1941. (*Z. Ridley via author*)

HMS *Devonshire*. Although undated, this photograph was taken after her 1950 refit, when the bridge HADT had been removed. Her armament comprises one twin 8 in and two twin 4 in. Also, there is a quad pom-pom to port and a single Bofors to starboard. Radar appears to be confined to Type 293 at the head of the foremast. The *Devonshire* had been converted to a training cruiser in 1947. Not only had her armament been reduced, but she also suffered the removal of all but four boilers, which brought her speed down to 21 kts. She was sold for scrap in 1954. (*Ian Allan / Science Museum / Science & Society S9925*)

HMS *Dorsetshire*. This undated photograph was probably taken in late 1941. The *Dorsetshire* wears a simple two-tone camouflage: most of the ship is dark, but the upper hull and upperworks around the bridge, third funnel and backs of A, and Y turrets are light. She is still in pre-war condition, with a sternwalk and two HADT abreast upper bridge. There are now four twin 4 in, with octuple pom-poms aft of the catapult and quad 0.5 in on platforms between the first and second funnels. She has no radar or 20 mm guns. The *Dorsetshire* was bombed on 5 April 1942. (*Ian Allan/Science Museum/Science & Society S1435*)

Dorsetshire Class Heavy Cruisers – two ships, first laid down in July 1927. Standard displacement 9,950 tons (av); length and beam 632ft 8 in x 66 ft; power 80,000 shp for 32.25 kts; principal armament: eight 8 in and four 4 in guns, eight 21 in torpedo tubes; protection: sides, 1 in (partial), deck 1.5 in (max) (partial).

HMS *Dorsetshire* (1929). On a standard Showing the Flag cruise, the *Dorsetshire* is at anchor in Stockholm Harbour in June 1931. Fairey IIIF S1507 '59' is on the catapult and a rear-admiral's flag is at the fore. Royal Marines in pith helmets are drawn up on the quarterdeck and by the port torpedo tubes. This small class received MkII 8 in turrets and improved magazine protection. They carried the same heavy DCT as the Yorks. (*Plymouth Naval Base Museum*)

HMS *Norfolk* (1928). In the foreground is the flight deck of USS *Ranger*, with Grumman Wildcat fighters ranged aft. The *Norfolk* is passing to port, off Akureyri in Iceland, on 17 October 1943 and at this time she has twelve single 20 mm in her light AA armament. The camouflage colours are believed to be mid blue, light blue and pale grey. By this time her standard displacement had grown to about 10,900 tons. During the Battle of North Cape she hastened the end of the *Scharnhorst* by putting her radar out of action with her 8 in guns. The *Norfolk* was sold for scrap in 1950. (*US National Archives 80-G-201168*)

York Class Heavy Cruisers – two ships, first laid down in May 1927. Standard displacement 8,400 (*York*), 8,550 (*Exeter*) tons; length and beam 575 ft x 57 ft (58 ft *Exeter*); power 80,000 shp for 32.25 kts; principal armament: six 8 in and four 4 in guns, six 21 in torpedo tubes; protection: sides, 3 in armour belt (partial), deck 3 in (max) (partial).

HMS *York* (1928). The presence of Fairey IIIF S1484 '57' of 443 Flight on her catapult dates this image of the *York* at early 1931. The sides ahead of the torpedo tubes have not been plated-in, and there is a total absence of light AA guns. Above X turret is the control top of a distant capital ship. She was the first ship to be fitted with the new 8 in DCT weighing over 11 tons. Although better protected than the Counties, these two ships had no other virtues. On 12 October 1940 she sank the destroyer RN *Artigliere*, which had been damaged earlier by HMS *Ajax*. The *York* was damaged, beached and abandoned on 26 March 1941. (*Ian Allan / Science Museum / Science & Society N1025*)

HMS *Exeter* (1929). The badly damaged *Exeter* is lying at Port Stanley in the Falkland Islands after Battle of the River Plate, where, flooding and with no guns in action, she had arrived on 16 December 1939. Damage and scorching along her starboard side from the bows to X turret are clearly visible. Both A and B turrets have been wrecked by direct hits by 28 cm shells from the *Admiral Graf Spee*, and the single 4 in guns are trained outboard, disabled. The bridge has been wrecked by the 28 cm hit on B turret, the second of five. The *Exeter* was a half-sister of the *York*, distinguishable by her vertical funnels and masts. She was sunk by gunfire and torpedoes on 1 March 1942. (*Plymouth Naval Base Museum*)

Leander Class Light Cruisers – five ships, first laid down in September 1930. Standard displacement 7,052 tons (av); length and beam 554 ft 6 in x 56 ft (55 ft Leander); power 72,000 shp for 32.5 kts; principal armament: eight 6 in and four 4 in guns, eight 21 in torpedo tubes; protection: sides 3 in armour belt on 1in hull plating (max) (partial), deck 2 in (max) (partial).

HMS *Achilles* (1932). Autumnal Mersey mists provide the backdrop for the *Achilles* in late September/early October 1933, when she is almost ready to be handed over to the Royal Navy. There are quad 0.5 in mountings, under dark canvas, in the bridge wings and above X turret. The aerial yard is hung, trapeze like, from the mainmast, which could be raised for improved communications. A catapult is yet to be fitted abaft the funnel. As built, this class was poorly equipped for gunnery control, having only a single DCT (the first pattern of the 6 in type) and HADT. The first light cruisers for over a decade, this was one of only two classes of metal-hulled true cruisers with a single funnel, the other being the Merseys of the 1880s. She was later loaned to New Zealand and eventually transferred to India. (*Cammell Laird Archives/Wirral Museum*)

HMS *Neptune* (1933). Unfortunately, this photograph has proved impossible to date, because the *Neptune* visited Simon's Town on several occasions between November 1937 and August 1939. Her secondary armament is now four twin 4 in, all in the positions around the funnel previously occupied by the original singles. She has a Seafox aircraft on the catapult. With the *Ajax* and *Penelope* she sank the destroyer RN *Alvise da Mosta* during successful air/sea operations against Italian convoys on 1 December 1941. The *Neptune* was mined on 19 December 1941. (*Simon's Town Museum*)

HMS *Ajax* (1934). At Alexandria in mid-1941, her catapult has been removed, to be replaced by a quad pom-pom. There are two light AA guns right aft which do not appear to be Oerlikons, and may therefore be captured Italian pieces. Otherwise, her light AA armament is still limited to three quad 0.5 in on the aft superstructure. The three-colour camouflage scheme resembles that on the *Capetown* (see p. 80). In December 1939 the *Ajax* had been flagship at the Battle of the River Plate, which led to the destruction of the Panzerschiffe (pocket battleship in popular parlance, although more akin to a pre-dreadnought armoured cruiser) *Admiral Graf Spee*. The *Ajax* was the first cruiser in Mediterranean with radar (Type 279), and on the night of 11/12 October 1940 this assisted her in sinking the fleet torpedo boats RN *Arione* and *Ariel*, and damaging the destroyers RN *Artigliere* and *Aviere*. The *Ajax* was sold for scrap in 1949. (*National Maritime Museum N31286*)

HMS *Orion* (1932). It is 24 April 1942, and the *Orion* is off Plymouth after a minor refit in which Type 273 radar, badly 'wooded' by the aft superstructure, has been installed, and camouflage applied. Close-range armament is now two quad pom-poms and seven single 20 mm, including one on each of B and X turrets. Splinter mattresses are on the aft searchlight platform. (*Plymouth Naval Base Museum*)

HMS *Orion*. As the LCI(M) HMCS *Prince David* enters the inner harbour at Piraeus on 10 November 1944, she is passing the *Orion*'s starboard side. She now wears a two-tone paint scheme in lieu of camouflage, but no other changes are apparent. The elderly Greek cruiser *Giorgios Averoff* (1910) 9,956t, to port, has a 3 in AA gun on the roof of the forward twin 9.2 in turret. The *Orion* was sold for scrap in 1949. (The *Averoff* is preserved at Poros.) (*D.J. Thorndick/DND/National Archives of Canada PA-142888*)

Arethusa Class Light Cruisers – four ships, first laid down in January 1933. Standard displacement 5,245 tons (av); length and beam 506 ft x 51 ft; power 64,000 shp for 32.25 kts; principal armament: six 6 in and four (*Aurora* and *Penelope* eight) 4 in guns, six 21 in torpedo tubes; protection: sides 2.25 in belt (max) (partial), deck 2 in (max) (partial).

HMS *Arethusa* (1934). During the first half of her commission as flagship of 3 CS in the Mediterranean the *Arethusa* carried a Hawker Osprey floatplane, as seen here. A second aircraft could be carried on the deckhouse aft of the second funnel. Awnings are spread extensively. The first two ships lacked an aft HADT. This class had been developed in parallel with the Amphions, of which they were diminutives. (*Simon's Town Museum*)

HMS *Arethusa*. The *Arethusa* is seen at speed in the Mediterranean on 8 May 1942, shortly after a refit which increased her armament to include four twin 4 in, two quad pom-poms and eight single 20 mm, together with radar Types 273, 281, 282, 284 and 285. She has also received a second HADT. The catapult had been removed much earlier. On 16 February 1940 the *Arethusa* had set in train a major morale-boosting operation, when she sighted the German auxiliary tanker *Altmark*, carrying prisoners from ships sunk by the *Admiral Graf Spee*. The *Arethusa* was sold for scrap in 1950. (*Portsmouth Royal Dockyard Historical Trust*)

HMS *Galatea* (1934). Riding at anchor in Scapa Flow in 1941, the *Galatea* is seen prior to her departure for the Mediterranean in July. She already has Type 279 radar and two quad pom-poms, but other close-range armament is confined to two quad 0.5 in by the forward funnel. Heavy seas have eroded the medium grey paint forward, revealing areas of earlier darker colour. The *Galatea* was torpedoed by *U557* on 15 December 1941. (*National Maritime Museum N31662*)

HMS *Aurora* (1936). Dating from about July 1943, this photograph of the *Aurora* was taken between the bombardment of Pantellaria on 8 June 1943 and Operation Husky (the invasion of Sicily) the following month. At this time she has two quad pom-poms and nine single 20 mm, including two on the quarterdeck. Radar includes Type 273 before the bridge. Earlier, with the *Penelope*, she sank an entire convoy and the destroyer RN *Fulmine* on 9 November 1941. She was later transferred to China. (*National Maritime Museum PM1173/1*)

Amphion Class Light Cruisers – three ships, first laid down in June 1933. Standard displacement 7,080 tons (av); length and beam 562 ft 3 in x 56 ft 8 in; power 72,000 shp for 32.5 kts; principal armament: eight 6 in and four 4 in guns, eight 21 in torpedo tubes; protection: sides 3 in belt on 1 in hull plating (max) (partial), deck 2 in (max) (partial).

HMS *Apollo* (1934). Seen from her own aircraft at emergency speed in February 1937, the *Apollo* is making for Martinique (in the distance), where a violent eruption had occurred. There is water on the quarterdeck. The revisions to this class brought twin funnels, an increase of some 8 ft in length and an elegance of profile when new that was probably unmatched. She was later transferred to Australia. (*Plymouth Naval Base Museum*)

HMS *Amphion* (1934). The *Amphion* carried Osprey aircraft from commissioning in mid-1936 to early 1938, which is the only clue we have for the date of this photograph. Two Ospreys of 716 Squadron are visible, one being hoisted in onto the catapult. Spare aircraft floats are stowed aft of second funnel. Developed from the Leander class, their rearranged machinery spaces were less vulnerable to underwater damage. She was also transferred to Australia. (*Ian Allan/Science Museum/Science & Society S1015*)

Southampton Class Light Cruisers – five ships, first laid down in October 1934. Standard displacement 9,057 tons (av); length and beam 591 ft 6 in x 61 ft 8 in; power 75,000 shp for 32 kts; principal armament: twelve 6 in and eight 4 in guns, six 21 in torpedo tubes; protection: sides 4.5 in belt (partial), deck 2 in (max) (partial).

HMS *Glasgow* (1936); see also frontispiece. The *Glasgow* is in 'as built' condition here, probably during 1937, with no HADT for the secondary armament and no shelters between the 4 in guns for the gun crews. The sun is astern on the starboard quarter, causing heavy shadows. This class and the Gloucesters were all originally fitted with a close-range armament of two quad pom-poms and two quad 0.5 in. They were triple-turret developments of the Amphions, their elegant looks marred only by the heavy hangars. (*Plymouth Naval Base Museum*)

HMS *Southampton* (1936). This early wartime photograph dates from before May 1940, because the *Southampton* still lacks her aft HADT. There is no radar fitted; instead there is a DF loop at the head of the foremast. However, she already has an external degaussing coil. The torpedo tubes are trained outboard. The *Southampton* was sunk by the Royal Navy after bomb damage on 11 January 1941. (*National Maritime Museum N6255*)

HMS *Newcastle* (1936). Taken sometime between April 1940 and April 1941, this image shows the *Newcastle* with UP launchers on B turret and the quarterdeck. Other signs of wartime modifications are the external degaussing coil and the Carley floats – in two sizes – on the hangar side. Watertight shutters are closed over the torpedo tubes. At the head of the foremast is an MF/DF aerial. There is no radar. (*Ian Allan / Science Museum / Science & Society N1015*)

HMS *Newcastle*. This photograph apparently dates from very late 1942, between the October/November refit in New York, when the Type 284 radar had been fitted, and her arrival at Devonport on 21 December, when an additional ten 20 mm were installed. Types 281 and, before the bridge, 273 had been fitted a year earlier, together with the nine single 20 mm. The ship's boats have not been moved to the catapult deck. The *Newcastle* was sold for scrap in 1959. (*Maritime Photo Library 1367*)

HMS *Sheffield* (1936). Photographed from a naval aircraft, the *Sheffield* is in Scapa Flow sometime between September 1941 and March 1942. Her close-range armament now includes six single Oerlikons, including those atop B and X turrets. The radar suite does not yet include Type 273 and the aft HADT, mounted low, lacks Type 285. She had been fitted with the Royal Navy's first radar set, an experimental Type 79Y, on 15 August 1938, using it operationally for the first time on 25 September 1939 in detecting an air attack on the Home Fleet in the North Sea. In the Battle of the Barents Sea she sank the destroyer *Friedrich Eckoldt* (*Z16*) and, with the *Jamaica*, drove off the heavy cruisers *Admiral Hipper* and *Lützow*, with serious damage to the former. (*Fleet Air Arm Museum CARS S/106*)

HMS *Sheffield*. This famous ship served much of her time post-war as a flagship; note the flagstaff at the head of the foremast. The *Sheffield* is seen here in 1953, when she participated in the Coronation Review at Spithead. Her close-range armament and sensors are of early post-war standard and would be upgraded later. As seen, she has two quad pom-poms, plus four twin and ten single Bofors. X turret was removed from the survivors of the class between 1944 and 1945. The fleet tender *MFV 1142* lies alongside. The *Sheffield* was sold for scrap in 1967. (*Ian Allan/Science Museum/Science & Society S9969*)

HMS *Birmingham* (1936). Wearing the flag of RAd Gladstone, Flag Officer 2i/c Far East Station, the *Birmingham* is seen arriving at Hong Kong on 3 October 1954. During modernization at Portsmouth the signal (hangar roof) deck has been lowered and she has been given a streamlined bridge to deflect nuclear blast, two AA/SU Mk6 plus associated Type 275 radar, and a lattice foremast carrying radar Types 277Q and 293Q. She also has Types 274 and 281B plus its IFF. There is a YE-60 beacon on the aft superstructure. Close-range armament comprises six twin and six single Bofors. She had seen operational service between 1952 and 1953 during the Korean War, and later starred in the film *The Baby and the Battleship*. The only cruiser since the Carlisles of 1917 to not feature a knuckle at the bow, she was sold for scrap in 1960. (*Public Record Office ADM 1/25564*)

Gloucester Class Light Cruisers – three ships, first laid down in February 1936. Standard displacement 9,394 tons; length and beam 591 ft 6 in x 62 ft 4 in; power 82,500 shp for 32.25 kts; principal armament: twelve 6 in and eight 4 in guns, six 21 in torpedo tubes; protection: sides 4.5 in belt (partial), deck 2 in (max) (partial).

HMS *Gloucester* (1937). Photographed in Grand Harbour, Malta, during 1941, the *Gloucester*'s camouflage scheme appears to contain only two colours. Typical of the time and place, radar is limited to Type 279: there are no enhancements to her AA armament. The second DCT aft, a characteristic of these three ships, is just visible behind the aft HADT. Another characteristic is the rounded bridge front. Their protection also featured detail improvements. The *Gloucester* was bombed on 22 May 1941. (*National Maritime Museum N31677*)

HMS *Manchester* (1936). Operating with the Home Fleet in May 1942, the *Manchester* is painted in Mountbatten Pink. There is a Bofors gun on B turret and eight single 20 mm have replaced the original 0.5 in. Radar includes Types 273 (abaft the forward DCT with its Type 284), 279 and 285 (not on the aft HADT). A Supermarine Walrus amphibian sits on the catapult deck. The *Manchester* was sunk by the Royal Navy after torpedo damage on 13 August 1942. (*Fleet Air Arm Museum CARS M/42*)

HMS *Liverpool* (1937). This private snapshot shows the *Liverpool* shortly after being hit by an air-launched torpedo on 14 June 1942, during Operation Harpoon (Malta convoy). She is under tow without power and is listing about 7°. Incredibly, she was under repair for the rest of the war. She was an unlucky ship, which missed two-thirds of the war because of action damage. Her camouflage scheme is an Admiralty Light Pattern: standard light grey with medium and dark blue and grey patches added. (*J.P. Daley via author*)

HMS *Liverpool*. Most of her post-war service was spent in the Mediterranean, mainly as flagship of 1 CS, and where this photograph was taken in June 1951. The *Liverpool* now has a close-range battery of six quad pom-poms and ten single Bofors, including six on the catapult deck. Her aft DCT has been landed, along with X turret. The parabolic dish of the Type 277 radar is on a tower aft of the DCT, and there are remnants of Type 650 missile-jammers on the mainmast, which itself is surmounted by Type 279B. By this time her tonnage had increased by some 10 per cent. The *Liverpool* was sold for scrap in 1958. (*Maritime Photo Library 1392*)

Edinburgh Class Light Cruisers – two ships, first laid down in December 1936. Standard displacement 10,485 tons (av); length and beam 613 ft 6 in x 63 ft 4 in; power 80,000 shp for 32.5 kts; principal armament: twelve 6 in and twelve 4 in guns, six 21 in torpedo tubes; protection: sides 4.5 in belt (partial), deck 3 in (max) (partial).

HMS *Edinburgh* (1938). The six single 20 mm guns seen here – two on B turret, two on B gun deck and two right aft – were added in July 1941, before the *Edinburgh* took part in Operation Substance (Malta convoy). The sailors in shorts place the location in the Mediterranean. There is radar Type 279 at the mastheads. The *Edinburgh* was sunk by the Royal Navy after torpedo damage, having sunk the German destroyer *Hermann Schoemann* (*Z7*), on 2 May 1942. (*National Maritime Museum A6434*)

HMS *Belfast* (1938). In dry dock at Portsmouth, the *Belfast* is undergoing her 1999 refit. Preserved instead of the more appropriate *Sheffield*, she is a 1930s hull and principal armament, topped by late-1950s equipment and fittings. The 1940s four-colour camouflage scheme is totally inappropriate to her configuration. On 21 November 1939 her back was broken by a magnetic mine. During reconstruction the hull had to be encased in a special strengthening bulge, which increased her beam to 66 ft 4 in, the close-range armament was enhanced and radar was fitted. Later, she landed two of her twin 4 in mountings. Between 1956 and 1959 she was extensively modernized to her present appearance. Changes included an enlarged bridge, two lattice masts, a homogeneous battery of six twin Bofors MkV mountings, new individual MRS8 directors for these and the 4 in, and an updated radar outfit of Types 262, 274, 277Q, 293Q, 960 (which appears to lack its complimentary Type X IFF) and 968. As a result, standard displacement rose to 11,550 tons and speed fell to about 31 kts. (*Royal Navy*)

5 REARMAMENT, FURTHER STRIFE AND THE END OF THE LINE

The Didos and Fijis were the first new designs after rearmament was belatedly and reluctantly accepted. Although the Dido class dual-purpose cruisers did much good work, their 5.25 in turrets were too cramped to allow the expected rate of high-angle fire to be sustained. They nevertheless frequently punched above their weight. The Bellonas were their half-sisters.

Similarly armed to the preceding Towns, the Fijis, which introduced the transom stern, were designed within the 8,000 ton limit set by the 1936 London Naval Treaty – a limit to which no other nation adhered. Two were cancelled and three, with X turret replaced by a quad pom-pom, became the Uganda class.

Thirteen Minotaur class ships, a 63 ft beam development of the Fiji concept, were projected. They were the *Bellerophon*, *Minotaur* and *Swiftsure* (1941 programme), *Defence*, *Superb* and *Tiger* (1941 supplementary programme), *Blake*, *Hawke* and one not named before cancellation (1942 programme). The remaining four were not ordered. In 1945 the *Blake* briefly exchanged names with the *Tiger* before reverting. Then, also in 1945, the *Bellerophon* became *Tiger*, the *Minotaur* became *Ontario*, and the original *Tiger* had her name changed again, becoming *Bellerophon*. She and the unnamed ship were then cancelled. The partially completed *Hawke* was cancelled and broken up on slip post-war. In 1957 the *Defence*, one of three laid up incomplete, was renamed *Lion*. Designed in the light of experience, these ships had an enhanced AA armament, but planned weight continued to rise and all but the first two ships to complete were redesigned with a 64 ft beam, becoming the Tiger class.

The United Kingdom was impoverished after the war and the several schemes for brand new cruisers were a waste of paper, as had been the Second World War plans for the Admiral and Neptune classes. During the war, air raids, limited shipyard facilities and a shortage of equipment affected repairs and refitting at home, and the developing need to upgrade radar and AA armament was constantly hampered by a lack of resources. Fortunately, the United States was able to undertake many vital wartime tasks. These and post-war refits and modifications were generally on an *ad*

Dido Class Light Cruisers – eleven ships, first laid down in August 1937. Standard displacement 5,624 tons (av); length and beam 512 ft x 50 ft 6 in; power 62,000 shp for 32.25 kts; principal armament: ten 5.25 in guns, six 21 in torpedo tubes; protection: sides 3 in belt (max) (partial), deck 2 in (max) (partial).

HMS *Bonaventure* (1939). The first Dido class to complete (and the first to be lost), the *Bonaventure* is seen on 4 October 1940, travelling in the wake of her sistership *Naiad*, while serving with the Home Fleet. A shortage of 5.25 in turrets let to the fitting of a 4 in starshell gun in X position. Radar is confined to Type 279 and, unfortunately, the aerials have been subjected to some crude retouching. Her unpainted wooden decks stand out clearly. The class was developed from the Arethusas. All these ships had a special 5.25 in DCT and were completed with two quad pom-poms, and in addition the *Bonaventure* has two quad 0.5 in. The *Bonaventure* was torpedoed by the Italian submarine *Ambra* on 31 January 1941. (*Business Records Centre, University of Glasgow*)

hoc basis, leading to a heterogeneous mix of weapons and equipment within classes. Additional AA weapons and radar added so much top-weight that, unlike those of other navies, many British cruisers had to land X turret to preserve stability. It was fortunate that radar allowed the landing of aircraft, catapults and associated equipment, thus saving valuable weight, although some ships inexplicably retained two cranes. Post-war, only the *Birmingham*, *Newcastle*, *Belfast*, *Newfoundland* and *Royalist* underwent partial modernization, but this did not include their main armament. The last conventional cruiser, HMS *Superb*, entered service post-war, but was laid up in only 1957 virtually unaltered.

The three laid-up ships were eventually completed to a much-modified and not entirely successful design with automatic 6 in and 3 in guns. Two of these were eventually converted into hybrid helicopter-carrying cruisers. These became the only British cruisers to carry guided missiles. Ironically, these two ships were withdrawn from service just before they could have been of great use in the 1982 liberation of the Falkland Islands.

During the first half of the Second World War, cruiser work followed fairly traditional lines. There were anti-raider patrols and trade protection duties from day one. In the West, German ships offered few opportunities for combat. For the British navies

HMS *Phoebe* (1939). In this scene off Alexandria in about mid-1941, the destroyer *Janus* (*G53*) is about to pass down the *Phoebe*'s starboard side. The cruiser is in original condition and has the same radar and armament as the *Bonaventure*, but with the 4 in gun in C position, instead of X. The *Phoebe* was sold for scrap in 1956. (*National Maritime Museum N31757*)

the cruiser *v.* cruiser war was fought mainly in the Mediterranean. Here, the small Arethusas and Didos proved popular and successful. In the Far East, Japan's preponderance in carriers and 8 in cruisers (including eight of over 13,000 tons) caused such major problems at a time when the newest and strongest ships were in the North Atlantic or Mediterranean, that opportunities for successful action were elusive. Later, by the time more capable resources could be spared and the weak Eastern Fleet had been transformed into the East Indies and British Pacific Fleets, the principal duties of cruisers were AA protection for carrier groups and occasional shore bombardments. The same was true later, during the Korean War, for which six cruisers were awarded the battle honour Korea, and Malayan Emergency of the 1950s.

Mines and shell fire proved less damaging than torpedoes and bombs, the efficiency of German and Japanese dive-bombers and of Italian torpedo-bombers coming as particularly nasty shocks. Inevitably, the smallest cruisers were the least able to absorb severe damage.

Post-war, the surviving cruisers of the Southampton and later classes remained in ever-decreasing numbers, but older ships were largely worn out and most were disposed of by 1950. Their duties included the traditional tasks of providing disaster relief and transporting troops at speed to trouble spots against insurrections and riots. The 1953 Coronation Review was the last substantial gathering of British and Commonwealth cruisers, some being dragged out of cocooned retirement for the event. The last conventional ships were laid up by the mid-1960s, and by 1977 and the Silver Jubilee Review, as always at Spithead, the two converted Tigers were all that remained.

HMS *Euryalus* (1939). Newly completed at Chatham, the *Euryalus* is a bizarre sight. Such complicated multi-coloured camouflage schemes (even the boats are camouflaged) were largely ineffective: at the time another was worn by the *Cleopatra*. As yet she is sparsely provided with modern equipment. Her additional AA armament is confined to two quad 0.5 in and,

although she has radar Types 279 and 284, the aft HADT has the only 285 set. A large diamond-shaped HF/DF aerial is built on to the mainmast. (*Public Record Office ADM 176/247*)

HMS *Euryalus*. Twelve years later, while visiting Simon's Town in 1953, the *Euryalus* reveals her wartime changes, most prominent of which is the replacement of C turret by a third quad pom-pom. She is wearing the flag of CinC South Atlantic, even though these cramped ships made poor flagships. In 1959 she was the last of the class to be sold for scrap. (*Simon's Town Museum*)

HMS *Argonaut* (1941). The *Argonaut*, the last Dido class to complete, is in new condition in August 1942. Apart from the standard pom-poms her AA armament is confined to four single 20 mm. There is an HF/DF aerial between the funnels, in line with the starboard pom-pom director and its Type 282 radar. Colours are believed to be dark grey/green, white and some light blue. On 2 December 1942, with the *Aurora*, *Sirius* and destroyers of Force Q, she sank all four MVs in Italian convoy, together with destroyer RN *Folgore*, near the Skerki Bank. She was sold for scrap in 1955. (*Cammell Laird Archives/Wirral Museum*)

HMS *Dido* (1939). Having refitted at Liverpool in 1943, the *Dido* is now in her final wartime configuration. She has the standard mid-war radar outfit, including lightweight Type 272, and her close-range armament now includes four twin and two single 20 mm. There is an MF/DF aerial amidships: the external degaussing coil had been fitted earlier. The dark section of the two-colour paint scheme includes A turret and the first funnel. She was not refitted with the latest electronics post-war, because the five turret ships were too top-heavy. Earlier, the *Dido* had received the fleet's first Type 281 air-warning radar in October 1940. She was sold for scrap in 1958. (*Cammell Laird Archives/Wirral Museum*)

HMS *Sirius* (1940). The *Sirius* is seen from a naval aircraft in 1943, steaming at 20 kts while serving with Force H in the Mediterranean. Radar includes Type 272 on the foremast starfish. She appears to be as built, with five single 20 mm guns. The *Sirius* was the last large warship completed at Portsmouth, where bombing had delayed her completion until May 1942. (*Fleet Air Arm Museum CARS S/110*)

HMS *Sirius*. This later photograph of the *Sirius* dates from the winter of 1947/48, when she was temporarily laid up in Scottish waters. She has Type 243 IFF at the head of the mainmast and a standard diamond-shaped HF/DF aerial between the funnels, but she could not be refitted with the most modern weapons and electronics because of topweight problems. In addition to two quad pom-poms her close-range armament includes four single Bofors. Being cramped and weight-sensitive, the Didos were of very limited value to the post-war navy. The *Sirius* was sold for scrap in 1956. (*Ian Allan/Science Museum/Science & Society S2925*)

HMS *Cleopatra* (1940). The *Cleopatra* makes an interesting comparison with the previous plate. Her weapons and sensors are more modern than those of the *Sirius*, because she has lost C turret and has three US-pattern quad Bofors and six twin 20 mm. The radar now includes Types 277 and 293 on foremast and 242 and 281B at head of mainmast. Like the *Sirius*, she too is laid up in Scottish waters during 1947/48. Except that her paint scheme now lacks a blue waterline panel, her appearance is unaltered since the end of war service with the East Indies Fleet. The *Cleopatra* was sold for scrap in 1958. (*Ian Allan/Science Museum/Science & Society S2930*)

HMS *Scylla* (1940). Operating off Italy as part of Force H during the Salerno Campaign, the *Scylla* is seen in September 1943. A squadron of RAF Beaufighters passes overhead. A shortfall in production of 5.25 in turrets affected many Dido class ships. The *Scylla* and her sistership the *Charybdis* were modified to carry an extemporized main armament of eight 4.5 in twin mountings of the type used in the *Ark Royal*. By this date close-range armament is two quad pom-poms and twenty 20 mm (six twin and eight single). The radar suite includes Type 272 at the foremast starfish, and she has two HADTs but no DCT. The camouflage is patches of light blue, white and dark grey/green. The *Scylla* was sold for scrap in 1950. (*Fleet Air Arm Museum CARS S/108*)

Fiji Class Light Cruisers – eight ships, first laid down in February 1938. Standard displacement 8,530 tons; length and beam 555 ft 6 in x 62 ft; power 80,000 shp for 32.25 kts; principal armament: twelve 6 in and eight 4 in guns, six 21 in torpedo tubes; protection: sides 3.5 in belt (max) (partial), deck 2 in (max) (partial).

HMS *Trinidad* (1940). Built at Devonport, the new *Trinidad* is lying off Plymouth on completion in October 1941. An MF/DF aerial is on a bracket on the bridge front, the preferred position in larger ships. The whole class completed with three HADT to control AA fire, plus two quad pom-poms. In addition the *Trinidad*, the fifth ship to complete, had four quad 0.5 in machine-guns. To save topweight the control position on X turret was fitted in all in lieu of a much heavier aft DCT. On 29 March 1942, while escorting convoy PQ13, she sank the German destroyer *Z26*. The *Trinidad* was sunk by the Royal Navy on 15 May 1942 after bomb damage. (*Plymouth Naval Base Museum*)

HMS *Mauritius* (1939). After her first refit the *Mauritius* is off Plymouth on 3 April 1942. Work has included adding four 20 mm guns (two in the bridge wings and two on quarterdeck), together with radar Type 273 on the bridge front. A Walrus aircraft is in launching position on the catapult. The top of the breakwater lighthouse appears above X turret. The *Mauritius* was sold for scrap in 1965. (*Plymouth Naval Base Museum*)

HMS *Jamaica* (1940). Photographed in 1942/43, the *Jamaica* has received only a few additional 20 mm guns since completion. Positions for at least eight and possibly ten can be identified. Radar includes Type 273 before the bridge, but there is no Type 285 on the aft HADT (it could have been a victim of the censor). Colours are believed to be dark grey, light blue and pale grey. It was in this condition that she and the *Sheffield* bested the *Admiral Hipper* (14,247 tons, eight 20.3 cm) and *Lützow* (11,700 tons, six 28 cm and eight 15 cm), during the Battle of the Barents Sea on 31 December 1942. (*Ian Allan / Science Museum / Science & Society S1659*)

HMS *Jamaica*. This August 1945 image captures the *Jamaica* shortly after taking HM the King to the Channel Islands and just prior to joining 5 CS in the East Indies. Close-range armament is difficult to identify, but includes five quad pom-poms, and there appear to be four singles, plus four twin and six single Oerlikons. She carries a YE-60 beacon on a mast before the second funnel. The *Jamaica* had a successful deployment during the Korean War. With HMS *Belfast*, she took part in the first naval operation of the war on 30 June 1950. On 7 July she engaged three Communist torpedo boats off the east coast of Korea, sinking one, in the only surface action of the war. Then on 17 September she became the first United Nations ship to shoot down an enemy aircraft. As in other survivors of this class, X turret had been landed. The *Jamaica* was sold for scrap in 1960. (*Maritime Photo Library 1441*)

HMS *Kenya* (1939). Photographed in July 1945, the *Kenya* has recently returned from service with the East Indies Fleet. At this time she is probably the most up-to-date cruiser in the Royal Navy, having received an outfit of the new MkV twin Bofors; five of these plus eight singles (two of them on the catapult deck) comprise the very modern close-range armament. This had been fitted at Simon's Town in April 1945, when X turret was removed. There is only one crane. She was one of only three cruisers considered to have 'fair' air-warning radar immediately after the war, by when even Type 277 was considered out of date. She was sold for scrap in 1962. (*Maritime Photo Library 1443*)

HMS *Bermuda* (1941). Flagship of 5 CS in the Far East, the *Bermuda* is *en route* from Yokohama to Hong Kong in July 1946. Formerly a unit of the British Pacific Fleet, she retains her wartime appearance. Her radar outfit is similar to that of the *Kenya*: note the barrage directors with Type 283 before the bridge, and in addition she has an MF/DF aerial on a mast above it. The close-range armament is heavy but diverse, comprising five quad and four single pom-poms, two twin and two single 20 mm, plus a single Bofors each side of the catapult deck and the aft HADT. She has one crane and no torpedo tubes. (*Fleet Air Arm Museum CARS B/114*)

HMS *Bermuda*. The setting is the Kiel Canal, through which the *Bermuda* is passing in June 1960. She is flying the flag of Flag Officer Flotillas. She now has four lightweight MRS8 directors in place of the three heavier HADT MkIV, with radar Type 903 on the 4 in gun shields and Type 960 on the mainmast. However, the radar on the foremast is as before. Close-rang

armament is now seven MkV twin Bofors. Pennant numbers, in this case C52, were not worn on Royal Navy cruisers before the mid-1950s. The *Bermuda* was one of the last conventional cruisers to serve at sea. She was sold for scrap in 1965. (*Portsmouth Royal Dockyard Historical Trust*)

Uganda Class   Light Cruisers – three ships, first laid down in April 1939. Standard displacement 8,800 tons; length and beam 555 ft 6 in x 62 ft; power 80,000 shp for 32.25 kts; principal armament: nine 6 in and eight 4 in guns, six 21 in torpedo tubes; protection: sides 3.5 in belt (max) (partial), deck 2 in (max) (partial).

HMS *Ceylon* (1942). Newly completed, the *Ceylon* rides at anchor at Tail of the Bank, off Greenock, in July 1943. This class differed from the Fijis in being built with a third quad pom-pom in place of X turret. In addition there are eight twin 20 mm. Also, there is but a single crane. The DCT has been raised to clear the Type 272 lantern on the bridge. Colours appear to be light grey, pale blue and dark grey/green. The ten Carley floats are noteworthy. (*Business Records Centre, University of Glasgow*)

HMS *Ceylon*. Operations during the Korean War encountered extreme weather conditions, as the ice around the *Ceylon* testifies. She served with the United Nations force in that conflict between 1950 and 1952, undertaking several shore bombardments. Prior to deployment, Type 277 radar was installed aft and additional single Bofors replaced 20 mm mountings. She was later transferred to Peru. (*National Maritime Museum P69639*)

HMS *Newfoundland* (1941). With the *Mauritius* (C80) inboard, the *Newfoundland* (C59) is alongside at Portsmouth in about 1958/59, awaiting transfer to Peru at the end of 1959. She had been modernized in 1951/52 on similar lines to HMS *Birmingham*, but received two lattice masts. Almost hidden behind the mainmast is a YE-60 beacon, and totally hidden are two barrage directors side by side before the bridge. Her light AA armament comprises five twin and two single Bofors. She was involved in the only surface action of the Suez Campaign (Operation Musketeer) on 1 November 1956, when she sank the Egyptian frigate *Domiat*. The *Mauritius* remains in late-1940s condition. Outboard is a Ford class seaward defence boat. (*Ian Allan/Science Museum/Science & Society S2539*)

Bellona Class Light Cruisers – five ships, first laid down November 1939. Standard displacement 5,950 tons; length and beam 512 ft x 50 ft 6 in; power 62,000 shp for 32.25 kts; principal armament: eight 5.25 in guns, six 21 in torpedo tubes; protection: sides 3 in belt on 0.73 in hull plating (max) (partial), deck 2 in (max) (partial).

HMS *Spartan* (1942). Newly completed, the *Spartan* lies off Barrow in August 1943. She has a close-range armament of three quad pom-poms and six twin 20 mm, and is painted in light blue, white (the two almost indistinguishable in places) and dark grey/green, the standard colours for Didos and Bellonas. She was sunk by a German Hs-293A guided missile off Anzio on 29 January 1944. (*VSEL*)

HMS *Royalist* (1942). Lying at Tail of the Bank on 9 September 1943, the *Royalist* is complete as designed and is awaiting modification as an escort carrier group flagship. Close-range armament comprises three quad pom-poms and six twin 20 mm. Her camouflage is believed to comprise patches of light blue, dark grey/green and white. She was later loaned to New Zealand. (*Business Records Centre, University of Glasgow*)

HMS *Black Prince* (1942). Forming part of their anti-aircraft screen, the *Black Prince* is escorting fast carriers of the British Pacific Fleet off Okinawa on 1 April 1945, during Operation Iceberg. She has shot down a would-be suicide aircraft, which has crashed between her and HMS *Victorious*, its bomb creating a huge explosion. The 5.25 in cruisers were highly regarded as anti-Kamikaze escorts. She was later loaned to New Zealand. (*Public Records Office ADM 199/595*)

HMS *Diadem* (1942). Like some of the Didos post-war, the *Diadem* is seen laid up in Scottish waters in 1948, during one of the Royal Navy's periods of enforced austerity. Except that saluting guns have displaced four single 20 mm, she is little changed since her 1945 repairs. Her close-range armament comprises three quad pom-poms, eight twin 20 mm (four abreast the first funnel) and two singles. Her radar has not been updated. She was later transferred to Pakistan. (*Ian Allan/Science Museum/Science & Society S2927*)

Minotaur Class Light Cruisers – three ships in original programme, one subsequently modified to Tiger class, first laid down in September 1941. Standard displacement 9,100 tons; length and beam 555 ft 6 in x 63 ft; power 80,000 shp for 32.25 kts; principal armament: nine 6 in and ten 4 in guns, six 21 in torpedo tubes; protection: sides 3.5 in belt (partial), deck 2 in (max) (partial).

HMS *Swiftsure* (1943). This view of the *Swiftsure*, the newest cruiser to serve operationally in the Second World War, shows her leaving the Vickers Tyne shipyard in June 1944. For no apparent reason, especially as the radar remains untouched, the wartime censor has clumsily removed most of the land background. Confusingly, small areas of background remain above the extreme bow and around Y turret. The class benefited from a better AA armament than earlier ships, having an extra twin 4 in aft and four quad pom-poms, plus eight twin and six single Oerlikons. The *Swiftsure* was the first cruiser to receive Type 274 gunnery radar on the DCT. Otherwise, there is the standard late-wartime radar outfit. Beam was increased to 63 ft to compensate for additional top weight. (*Ian Allan/Science Museum/Science & Society S1654*)

HMS *Swiftsure*. The *Swiftsure* was refitted between 1950 and 1953, emerging in this configuration. Apart from the paint scheme the most noticeable change is the homogeneous close-range battery of four twin and nine single Bofors guns. Very few other changes are evident, although she does now have IFF at the mastheads. She is flying the flag of Flag Officer Flotillas. In 1962 she was sold for scrap. (*Ian Allan/Science Museum/Science & Society S9974*)

Tiger Class   Light Cruisers – four ships laid down, first in June 1942, plus one modified from Minotaur class. Standard displacement 9,400 tons; beam 64 ft; power 80,000 shp for 31.5 kts; principal armament: nine 6 in and ten 4 in guns, six 21 in torpedo tubes; protection: sides 3.5 in belt (partial), deck 2 in (max) (partial).

HMS *Hawke* (not launched). This enigmatic ship had been laid down on 1 July 1943 and was quite recognizable as a ship when cancelled. The incomplete hull fills the left-hand centreground, and the large casting is the *Hawke*'s rudder post, about to be positioned in this 1944 view of the famous Portsmouth building slip. She had even been allocated pennant number C27, but was suspended in January 1945. Finally cancelled in March 1946, she was broken up *in situ*. (*National Maritime Museum N25432*)

HMS *Superb* (1943). Still almost intact after being laid up in Gareloch for three years, the *Superb* (C25) is seen in July 1960, awaiting disposal. In this class further weight increases required another 1 ft increase in beam. She had been completed with three modern HADT MkVI, with their Type 275 radar, from the outset. However, despite being the newest conventional cruiser, she retained quad pom-poms, rather than twin Bofors, to the end of her days. Except for the substitution of Type 281B for her original Type 279B, the sensor suite also appears to be of 1945 vintage. The *Superb* was sold for scrap in 1960. (*Maritime Photo Library 1457*)

Tiger Class Three suspended ships completed to a revised design – the first suspended ship was taken in hand for conversion in 1954. Standard displacement 9,950 tons; length, beam and power as originally; principal armament: four 6 in and six 3 in guns; protection as originally.

HMS *Lion* (1944). This aerial view shows the *Lion* (C34) in 1961/62, the various awnings and the crew in shorts suggesting a tropical setting. Each of the five turrets (two Mk26 automatic twin 6 in and three Mk6 automatic twin 3 in) is controlled via its own dedicated MRS3 director, each with a dish aerial for Type 903 radar. These turrets were troublesome in service and failed to deliver the designed rate of sustained fire. Other sensors include Types 277Q, 960 (with, below it, the oblong aerial of the associated Type X IFF) and 992. Originally named the *Defence*, she had been rechristened in 1957. A shortage of both naval manpower and helicopters ruled out conversion to a command/helicopter cruiser and she was sold for scrap in 1972. (*Portsmouth Royal Dockyard Historical Trust*)

HMS *Tiger* (1945). Ordered as the *Bellerophon* (C20) of the 63 ft beam Minotaur class, it had been decided in 1943 to increase her beam to 64 ft, thereby making her a member of the Tiger class. The original *Tiger*, name-ship of class, was cancelled before being laid down, and this ship became the new *Tiger*, her name, but not her pennant number, being changed in 1945. Resembling the *Lion* on completion, she was converted to a command/helicopter cruiser (CCH) at Devonport between 1968 and 1972, with a flight deck and hangar for four Sea King anti-submarine helicopters. Among other changes, the midships 3 in guns were replaced by two quadruple launchers for Seacat guided missiles, utilizing the existing MRS3 directors. Her mainmast was plated over for strength to carry the large aerial for Type 965, plus Type 278, which replaced 277Q but used the same aerial. Note the tall funnels. She is ammunitioning from a supply ship on her starboard side. The conversion increased her overall length by 11 ft and standard displacement to 9,975 tons. Speed was reduced to about 30 kts. Although paid off in 1978, the *Tiger* did not go to the breakers until 1986, thus ending the era of the cruiser in the Royal Navy. (*Plymouth Naval Base Museum*)

6 OTHER NAVIES, OTHER FLAGS

Australia:	*The Royal Australian Navy*	New Zealand:	*The Royal New Zealand Navy*
Canada:	*The Royal Canadian Navy*	Pakistan:	*The Pakistani Navy*
		Peru:	*The Peruvian Navy*
China:	*The Chinese Navy*		
		Poland:	*The Polish Navy*
India:	*The Royal Indian Navy / Indian Navy*	South Africa:	*The South African Navy*

It was of course inevitable that those Old Commonwealth navies large enough to operate cruisers should use British-built, or, in the case of Australia, home-built examples of British-designed ships. During the two world wars many of these vessels operated as integral parts of British and Allied formations worldwide, doing invaluable work. The newly independent India and Pakistan also operated ex-Royal Navy ships.

The Chinese Navy selected HMS *Aurora* because no ship of a similar size and age was available elsewhere. It says much for the reputation of the design that the Peruvian Navy selected ships of the Uganda class at the end of the 1950s, when many surplus US Navy cruisers were available. On the other hand it has to be admitted that the ships which went to the Polish Navy did so because quite simply they were readily available.

AUSTRALIA

The Royal Australian Navy, the largest of the Commonwealth navies in the two world wars, was established on 5 October 1911, by way of the Commonwealth Naval Force, which had come into being on 1 March 1901. Given her geographical situation it was natural for Australia to acquire a cruiser force. Australia's indigenous shipbuilding industry was able to build small cruisers producing the pre-First World War design, *Brisbane* of the Chatham class, and *Adelaide* of the Birmingham class at Cockatoo Dockyard. Unfortunately, reliance on components imported from the UK, which was forced to give priority to naval construction programmes at home under wartime pressures, delayed completion of both, although the former did see service during the First World War. During 1915 the *Pelorus* class 3rd class protected cruiser *Psyche* transferred from New Zealand to Australian control. In both world wars Australian ships were in the thick of the fighting, operating alongside British and Allied forces in the North Sea, Mediterranean, Indian Ocean and Pacific

In the First World War all the cruisers saw service in far eastern waters, where the *Sydney* (Chatham class) won fame in her action against the elusive and troublesome *Emden*. She and the *Melbourne* later served with the Grand Fleet. There were grievous losses during the Second World War, resulting in heavy loss of life. First, the Amphion class light cruiser *Sydney* was sunk with all hands off Western Australia in an action against a Kriegsmarine auxiliary cruiser in November 1941, in which the latter was also sunk. Her sister ship *Perth* was the next to be lost, in one of the hopeless actions by combined Allied naval forces against the seemingly unstoppable Japanese advance in early 1942. Lastly, the *Canberra* had to be scuttled after receiving massive damage during the one-sided débâcle off Savo island in August of that year. The obsolete *Adelaide* saw only very limited service on such service as escorting local convoys.

Post war the Australians found their small and ageing cruiser force an expensive and increasingly irrelevant luxury. Although the ships survived into obsolescence longer than their Royal Navy counterparts, they languished inactive for most of their remaining years.

HMAS *Pioneer* (1899) Pelorus class. The sided 4 in guns on the *Pioneer*'s forecastle deck, typical of these diminutive cruisers, are clearly seen in this view, as is the embrasure for the main deck 3 pdr forward. Despite the many ventilation cowls, windsails are rigged aft of the second funnel. The *Pioneer* fired more rounds at the enemy in the First World War than any other Australian ship. She was paid off on 16 November 1916, but was not scuttled until 18 February 1931. (*Defence Public Affairs, Australia*)

HMAS *Encounter* (1902) Challenger class. Guns have been removed from the *Encounter*'s fighting tops, which are not completely circular, and have been replaced forward by a searchlight. A spotting top is now positioned at the head of her foremast, above which a small Australian ensign flies. Compared to the *Pioneer*, the lack of ventilation cowls gives a much more businesslike profile. The main armament includes two sided 6 in on the quarterdeck. Renamed the *Penguin* on 1 January 1923, she became a depot ship and was scuttled on 14 September 1932. (*Defence Public Affairs, Australia*)

HMAS *Sydney* (1912) Chatham class. Part of the Grand Fleet, the *Sydney* lies in the Firth of Forth in 1918, astern of units of the 2nd Battle Squadron. HMS *Erin* is directly ahead, then the *Centurion*, *Ajax* and, flying a kite balloon, the *King George V*. She suffered little damage in her successful duel with SMS *Emden* on 9 November 1914: her protection defeated enemy shells and she suffered only four dead and twelve wounded. Flagship of RAN between 1924 and 1927, she was broken up in 1929. (*Fleet Air Arm Museum CARS S/107*)

HMAS *Brisbane* (1915) Chatham class. Seen in Sydney Harbour in May 1920, the *Brisbane* is dressed overall to mark the visit of HRH the Prince of Wales. She has an empty searchlight platform on the foremast. Built in Australia and conceived as a 2nd class protected cruiser (belted), this ship was subsumed into the new light cruiser category before completion. After useful service in the First World War, she became a training ship in June 1928. She finally paid off at Portsmouth in September 1935, when her crew took over the new light cruiser *Sydney*. She was sold for scrap in 1936. (*Defence Public Affairs, Australia*)

HMAS *Melbourne* (1912) Chatham class. This post-war image of the *Melbourne* was captured in Australian waters, after she had landed the wartime aircraft flying-off platform and searchlight platform between the second and third funnels. Note the range clock on the foremast. She briefly became flagship of RAN from October 1927 to February 1928 vice HMAS *Sydney*, and was sold for scrap in 1928. (*Defence Public Affairs, Australia*)

HMAS *Adelaide* (1918) Birmingham class. This wartime photograph dates from prior to the *Adelaide*'s mid-1942 refit, during which radar was fitted. As seen, her AA armament is confined to three single 4 in guns, with the HADT on the foretop: there is not a single close-range gun. Built in Australia at a leisurely pace, she was conceived as a 2nd class protected cruiser (belted), but the new light cruiser category had been introduced before she was laid down in 1915. She was not completed until 1922, by when she was already obsolescent. The *Adelaide* lost her forward boiler room and first funnel in 1938/39, reducing her speed to 24 kts. She also landed one of the sided 6 in guns on the forecastle. She was sold for scrap in 1949. (*Defence Public Affairs, Australia*)

HMAS *Canberra* (1927) Kent class. Seen in about 1933 as flagship of the Royal Australian Navy, the *Canberra* wears a rear-admiral's flag at the fore. The single HADT is ahead of the mainmast, and before this there is a Supermarine Seagull III amphibian of 101 Fleet Co-operation Flight on the light SIIL catapult. The funnels of the two Australian Kents were 3 ft taller than those of their Royal Navy counterparts. (*Defence Public Affairs, Australia*)

HMAS *Canberra*. As part of Task Force 16, the *Canberra* is seen leaving Wellington, New Zealand, on 22 July 1942, *en route* to Guadalcanal and the disastrous action off Savo Island. Details of the ship are difficult to identify, but positions for seven or possibly nine 20 mm guns can be located. There is a vertical extension to the fore topmast, which could indicate the presence of Type 286 or 291 radar. Also, there is what appears to be Type 272 between the DCT and the foremast. The Allied cruiser force was surprised by the Japanese on the night of 8/9 August 1942 and, among other calamities, the *Canberra* was disabled by a number of 8 in shells. Her fate was sealed by a torpedo hit on her disengaged side, one recent theory being that this was a wild shot from a USN destroyer. Immobilized, she was sunk by USN later on 9 August. (*US National Archives 80-G-13454A*)

HMAS *Australia* (1927) Kent class. This rather fuzzy image shows the *Australia* at Sydney after her return from operations in Lingayen Gulf, when she gave AA and shore bombardment support for US landings in the Luzon area. Her high hull and three funnels made her a magnet for Kamikaze attacks. She survived six Kamikaze hits, including five within five days in January 1945. There were many casualties and these, coupled with a hit by a bomb-laden Mitsubishi Ki-46 Dinah on the waterline under the bridge (note scorching), and extensive serious superficial damage to funnels, AA armament, etc., forced her return to base. Although her exact close-range armament at this time is uncertain, there were two octuple pom-poms, at least ten Bofors mountings and at least eight 20 mm mountings, probably all singles. Radar includes Types 273 aft of the 284 equipped DCT. These many changes had raised her standard displacement to 11,051 tons. Her bows are off camera. She was sold for scrap in 1955. (*Australian War Memorial 019438*)

HMAS *Australia*. This dual image shows the aftermath in two areas of the ship of the January 1945 Kamikaze attacks. Many of the casualties were among the AA gun crews. In the left-hand frame is the demolished crane and the back of the damaged P2 twin 4 in (note exposed shells at left). Beyond P2 4 in can be seen three single Bofors, and the port pom-pom, with the barrels of X and Y turrets beyond. In the right-hand frame, even guard rails aft of Y turret have been damaged by blast from a bomb (from one of two Dinahs that hit the ship on 8 January) which exploded on the ship's side under the bridge, causing a 5° list. Stacked life rafts and a single Bofors are on the quarterdeck. (*Public Record Office ADM 267/81*)

HMAS *Shropshire* (1928) London class. With her crew manning the side the *Shropshire* is visiting Portsmouth in May 1946. In a 1945 refit she landed her torpedo tubes and received Type 277 radar and an enhanced close-range battery. Her AA armament now comprises four twin 4 in mountings, two octuple pom-poms, and eleven single Bofors. Transferred to RAN on 25 June 1943 as a replacement for the *Canberra*, HMAS *Shropshire* spent much of her war service supporting US amphibious operations in the Pacific. The catapult and aircraft arrangements were removed prior to transfer. She was sold for scrap in 1954. (*Royal Naval Museum, Portsmouth*)

HMAS *Sydney* (1934) Amphion class. During the action off Cape Spada on 19 July 1940 against the Italian light cruisers RN *Bartolomeo Colleoni* and *Giovanni della Bande Nere*, in which the former was sunk, the *Sydney* received a hit on the forward funnel. In addition, there appears to be some buckling of the stern plating. Here, she is at Alexandria on 21 July, undergoing repairs. The hospital ship *Maine* is ahead and HMS *Medway* is to starboard. She is in pre-war configuration, with single 4 in, no 20 mm guns and no radar. Earlier, on 28 June, she had sunk the destroyer RN *Espero*. Although built as HMS *Phaeton*, she did not serve under that name prior to being acquired by Australia. She was sunk in a mutually fatal duel with the German AMC *Kormoran* on 19 November 1941. (*Australian War Memorial 306697*)

HMAS *Hobart* (1934) Amphion class. On a glassy sea the *Hobart* is in typical Mediterranean camouflage. Her catapult had been landed in June 1941 and replaced by a single quad pom-pom, possibly from the *Perth*. She has no radar, but may have received a few Oerlikons. The weapon before the bridge may be one, or may be a captured Italian piece. It is not clear what guns are in the bridge wings, but she retains the quad 0.5 in ahead of X turret. She served in the Royal Navy as HMS *Apollo* before transfer to the RAN. (*Defence Public Affairs, Australia*)

HMAS *Hobart*. In this later view the *Hobart* is at Sydney on 20 December 1944, after an extensive post-damage refit. In this she received a greatly increased and effective close-range armament. This comprised two quad pom-poms amidships, a twin 20 mm on the aft superstructure ahead of X turret, three twin Bofors on Hazemeyer mountings, including one on the quarterdeck, and five singles. The radar outfit is also modern, and includes Types 276 and 277 on the foremast. The *Hobart* was sold for scrap in 1962. (*Australian War Memorial 084652*)

HMAS *Perth* (1934) Amphion class. This photograph may be the last clear image of the *Perth*. It was taken at Tanjong Priok on 28 February 1942, the day before she was overwhelmed and sunk in the Battle of Banten Bay, Java. Her Mediterranean camouflage has been overpainted, otherwise the only recent changes are the doubling of the 4 in armament to four twins, the replacement of two of her three quad 0.5 in by four single 20 mm guns, and the fitting of Type 286 HA/LA warning radar at the head of the mainmast. She retains her unique rangefinder baffles on her funnels. The *Perth* served with the Royal Navy as HMS *Amphion* before transfer. (*Defence Public Affairs, Australia*)

CANADA

The Royal Canadian Navy was established on 4 May 1910. Although her cruisers operated from the outbreak of the First World War, Canada found it difficult to maintain a cruiser force. In the Second World War, two modern ships were acquired, but prior to that a degree of Canadian manning had been applied to ships such as the cruiser *Enterprise*. Because the Canadian Government offered early release to many 'Hostilities Only' personnel, HMCS *Uganda* had embarrassingly to return to Canada in July 1945, while she was doing valuable service with the British Pacific Fleet, to land her crew. Post-war, many countries including Canada had difficulty in providing skilled crews to keep manpower-intensive ships such as cruisers in the front line, and the *Ontario* and *Quebec* became training ships.

HMCS *Rainbow* (1891) Apollo class. By the time this photograph was taken, on 8 January 1917, the *Rainbow* was relatively old. She is seen in Lyall Harbour, Saturna Island, in British Columbia. To the *Rainbow* fell the honour of being commissioned as the first unit of the Royal Canadian Navy on 4 August 1910. She spent the early years of the First World War in patrolling the western seaboard of North America, in August 1914 forming part of a squadron at Esquimalt with HMS *Newcastle* (flag) and HIJMS *Izumo*. The *Rainbow* was sold for mercantile use in 1920. (*Department of National Defence N-6365*)

HMCS *Niobe* (1897) Diadem class. Patrolling off the east coast of North America in June 1915, the *Niobe* makes a sight more impressive than the reality of her capabilities. Her port forecastle 6 in gun is trained outboard and numerous windsails are rigged. The false bow wave is typical of the period. In late August 1914 she had been manned by crews from sloops *Algerine* and *Shearwater* for service with 4 CS. Worn out, she became a depot ship in late 1915. Although her upperworks were wrecked in a major explosion at Halifax on 6 December 1917, she continued to serve until sold for scrap in 1920. (*Department of National Defence E-41058*)

HMCS *Aurora* (1913) Arethusa class. Alongside at Esquimalt in April 1921, the *Aurora* is seen with the destroyers HMCS *Patrician* and *Patriot*. The RCN was originally to have received HMS *Glasgow*, Bristol class, but the more modern and economical *Aurora* was substituted. She has the normal wartime modifications of the class, and retains the vestiges of an aircraft flying-off platform before the bridge. The *Aurora* was unique in having a single pom-pom on a raised platform (barely visible) aft of the after control position. She was sold for scrap in 1927. (*National Archives of Canada PA-115369*)

HMCS *Uganda* (1941) Uganda class. Photographed by a USN aircraft, the *Uganda*, one of the few ships to have yagi aerials on the DCT for Type 284 radar, is seen in November 1944 *en route* to the UK and thence to the British Pacific Fleet. She had been commissioned into the RCN on 21 October 1944 while in Charleston Navy Yard, USA, during repairs to damage sustained off Salerno on 13 September 1943. There she had been given an up-to-date radar outfit and a close-range armament, which included two US-pattern quad Bofors Mk2, plus associated directors, on the former catapult deck. As part of Task Force 57 the *Uganda* took part in the bombardment of Truk and escorted carriers off the Japanese mainland. However, operations in the Far East were curtailed by her recall to Canada before the end of the war. (*USN/National Archives of Canada* PA-107875)

HMCS *Quebec* (ex-*Uganda*). The *Quebec*, wearing pennant number 31, is coming alongside HMCS *Magnificent* on 15 May 1952 for the jackstay transfer of a rating to the carrier. By this time she was a training ship and her AA outfit had been reduced to a number of single Bofors only. She is in the standard RCN dark grey/light grey paint scheme, with the USN-style pennant number right forward. The *Uganda*, which had been rechristened HMCS *Quebec* on 14 January 1952, spent her post-war life off the Atlantic coast of Canada. (*Department of National Defence CT-852*)

HMCS *Quebec*. At the end of her life the *Quebec* is about to be towed from Halifax Dockyard by the tug *St John* on 30 September 1960, having paid-off on 13 June 1956. She has been stripped of all radar and armament except for the nine 6 in guns. Although in poor condition, she retains the red Maple Leaf emblem on the second funnel. The zareba for the former port quad Bofors and its director are clearly visible. In the foreground is the Canadian Tribal class destroyer *Micmac*. (*Department of National Defence HS-62657*)

HMCS *Ontario* (1943) Minotaur class. Leaving Valetta Harbour, Malta, on 23 July 1945, the *Ontario* is *en route* to join the British Pacific Fleet. In addition to the principal armament she carries the same close-range armament as her sister-ship the *Swiftsure* (p. 133): four quad pom-poms plus eight twin and six single Oerlikons. She was the first cruiser to take the new HADT MkVI, with its twin-aerial Type 275 radar, to sea, but she arrived in the Pacific too late to see action. Laid down as HMS *Minotaur*, she did not serve under that name, becoming the *Ontario* on commissioning into the Royal Canadian Navy at Harland & Wolff's Belfast yard on 26 April 1945. (*S.H. Draper/National Archives of Canada PA-136816*)

HMCS *Ontario*. A very smart-looking *Ontario*, displaying pennant number 32 and recently returned from representing Canada at the Coronation Fleet Review at Spithead that June, enters Vancouver Harbour in August 1953. Her radar outfit has been updated to include Type 277Q, while the close-range armament comprises four US-pattern quad Bofors Mk2 and seven singles, including one on the bridge front above B turret. In her rôle as West Coast training cruiser she was later partially disarmed. She was sold for scrap in 1960. (*National Archives of Canada PA-129227*)

CHINA

CS Chung King (1936) Arethusa class. The *Chung King* is arriving at Malta on 10 June 1948, *en route* to China under the command of Captain Tang Chow-hsiang. No apparent modifications were made before the *Aurora* was transferred to China at Portsmouth on 19 May 1948, the armament remaining at six 6 in, eight 4 in, two quad pom-poms and three twin 20 mm (one on X turret), plus two singles at the break of the forecastle, together with six 21 in torpedo tubes. After defecting to the Communists at Shanghai on 2 March 1949 and becoming the *Tchoungking*, *Tchoung King* or *Huang Ho* (evidence is contradictory), she was bombed by Nationalist B-24 aircraft and capsized off Calabash Island on about 20 March. She was later salvaged and served under a variety of names until about 1955, and was reputedly broken up in the 1960s. (*Royal Naval Museum, Portsmouth*)

INS *Delhi* (1932) Leander class. In this rare photograph the *Delhi* (C74) is nearing the end of her long life. The former HMS/HMNZS *Achilles* was commissioned as HMIS Delhi at Chatham on 5 July 1948. She served for exactly thirty years under the Indian flag, by when she had been in service for some forty-five years. Originally fleet flagship, having become INS *Delhi* on 26 January 1950, she was involved in the Goa Operation in December 1961, and became a training cruiser in August 1972, based at Cochin. For this rôle the forecastle deck has been extended to the former midships twin Bofors support and additional accommodation added above the former 4 in gun deck. Modern life rafts are stowed aft of this, and there appears to be a sail rigged at the mainmast, possibly to steady her at her mooring. The *Delhi* was paid off for disposal in 1978. (*Indian Navy*)

INS *Mysore* (1939) Fiji class. It is evident that someone is playing tricks, as the two outer guns in the *Mysore*'s B turret are elevated and disguised as missiles! In appearance she is very similar to the modernized *Newfoundland*, with two lattice masts and the former hangars cut down. Two modern AA/SU Mk6 control the 4 in guns, and the close-range armament comprises two single and five twin Bofors, with individual MRS8 directors for the latter. There are no torpedo tubes. The former HMS *Nigeria* had been commissioned as INS *Mysore* at Birkenhead on 29 August 1957 and in October became fleet flagship. She was engaged in operations in 1961, 1965 and 1971, and became a training cruiser in 1975. In 1986 she was sold for scrap. (*Indian Navy*)

NEW ZEALAND

The New Zealand Naval Force was established in 1914, and became the New Zealand Division of the Royal Navy on 20 June 1921. It was established as the Royal New Zealand Navy on 1 October 1941, but prior to that a number of cruisers had been New Zealand-manned and sailed under the New Zealand flag. A classic example was HMS *Achilles* at the Battle of the River Plate in 1939, but as early as 1914 a New Zealand Squadron, comprising the cruisers *Philomel*, *Psyche*, and *Pyramus* (the latter two being Pelorus class) was operating in the Pacific. After the Second World War the RNZN operated Bellona class cruisers for some years.

Pallas Class   3rd Class Protected Cruisers – nine ships, first laid down in August 1888. Legend displacement 2,575 tons; length and beam 278 ft x 41 ft; power 4,000 ihp for 17 kts; principal armament: eight 4.7 in guns, four 14 in torpedo tubes; protection: 2 in deck.

HMS *Philomel* (1890). The *Philomel*, wearing a false bow wave, is seen operating in the Red Sea in 1915. Awnings are rigged against the heat and large windsails and chimneys are seen fore and aft. A New Zealand ensign flies at the main topmast. Acquired as a seagoing training ship in 1914, she was activated for war service, and in August 1914 she formed part of the escort of the New Zealand Expedition to occupy Samoa. On 6 February 1915 she relieved the *Doris* off the Syrian coast. She paid off from operational service in 1917, but remained in service until 1946, eventually being scuttled in 1949. (*Royal New Zealand Navy Museum AAC 0020*)

HMS *Chatham* (1911) Chatham class. Seen as flagship at Auckland in 1922, the *Chatham* had been commissioned for New Zealand service in 1920 to replace the *Philomel* in front line service. It had not been possible to operate a newer ship because of a lack of oiling facilities. She served until 1924, when she was replaced by the *Dunedin* and rejoined the Royal Navy. In 1926 she was sold for scrap. (*Royal New Zealand Navy Museum GN 459/81*)

HMS *Dunedin* (1918) Delhi class. The *Dunedin* is off the town of Dunedin, New Zealand, in about 1930, having entered service in 1924. An oil tanker, the RFA *Nucula*, had to be acquired to support this oil-burning ship and her sister the *Diomede*. The two ships operated throughout the Pacific until their return to the Royal Navy. In the case of the *Dunedin*, this was in 1937, when she was replaced by the *Leander*. (*Royal New Zealand Navy Museum GN 3151/94*)

HMS *Diomede* (1919) Delhi class. Target practice was a constant requirement for all fighting ships, and the *Diomede* is moving her target, secured alongside her port bow, in this 1933 scene. By 1926 New Zealand's economic position had improved sufficiently for her to be acquired as a second oil-burning cruiser. The unique weatherproof gun house for No. one gun, which did not require No. two gun to have a blast deflector forward, is clearly visible. She returned to the Royal Navy in 1936. (*Royal New Zealand Navy Museum GN 210/94*)

HMNZS *Leander* (1931) Leander class. When photographed on 9 August 1942 the *Leander* had received no radar (the item before the funnel is probably a US-pattern HF/DF set) and few additional AA guns. The close-range armament is weak, with no pom-poms. There are six 20 mm guns: two singles right aft, two on the aft superstructure, vice two quad 0.5 in, and two in the bridge wings, but none on the turret roofs. One quad 0.5 in remains above X turret. Her colours are reputedly dark grey and dark grey/green. On 27 February 1941 she sank the Italian AMC *Ramb 1*. Later, she was badly damaged on 13 July 1943 during operations in support of US forces off the Solomon Islands. After long repairs she returned to the Royal Navy in 1945, and was sold for scrap in 1949. (*Royal New Zealand Navy Museum MN 29/89*)

HMNZS *Achilles* (1932) Leander class. Painted in the colours of the British Pacific Fleet, which she is *en route* to join, the *Achilles* is off Auckland in May 1945 after a refit. She displays the results of a full modernization at Portsmouth in 1943/44, when X turret had been landed and four twin 4 in and four quad pom-poms were fitted, together with a modern radar outfit. This includes Type 284 fed by yagi aerials on the DCT, behind which is Type 277. She had undergone the refit at Auckland between February and May 1945, when four Bofors were fitted in the bridge wings and the torpedo tubes landed. Close-range armament also includes at least three twin and four single 20 mm. She was the only ship in the British Pacific Fleet to have served throughout the six years of war. She had replaced the *Diomede* in 1936 and returned to the Royal Navy in 1946, later being transferred to India. The highlight of her long and interesting life was her part in the Battle of the River Plate against the *Admiral Graf Spee*. (*Royal New Zealand Navy Museum AAF 0195*)

HMNZS *Gambia* (1940) Fiji class. This photograph shows a scruffy-looking *Gambia* approaching Auckland in October 1944 for refit, during which radar Type 272 would be fitted to the platform on the foremast. Commissioned by a New Zealand crew on 22 September 1943, she was the first cruiser to enter New Zealand service as HMNZS although, for purely administrative reasons, the change of title did not take place until 8 May 1944. She returned to the Royal Navy in 1946, and was sold for scrap in 1968. (*Royal New Zealand Navy Museum AAI 037*)

HMNZS *Bellona* (1942) Bellona class. The unmistakable backdrop of Sydney Harbour Bridge frames the *Bellona* in this 1952 image. The only apparent changes are the addition of two twin 20 mm, making eight, and the deletion of all singles. She had been loaned to the RNZN in 1946 as one of two replacements for older 6 in cruisers, then later became a harbour training

ship at Auckland, and returned to Royal Navy control in 1956. She was sold for scrap in 1959. (*Royal New Zealand Navy Museum GN 1148/88*)

HMNZS *Black Prince* (1942) Bellona class. The *Black Prince* is approaching Auckland in about 1955, towards the end of her operational life. She has lost all pom-poms, plus their directors, and 20 mm guns, carrying instead ten single Bofors. The searchlights have also been landed but, surprisingly, the torpedo tubes remain. Air-warning radar has been upgraded to Type 281B, while Type 277 has replaced Type 272. With the *Bellona* she had entered RNZN service in 1946, and she was sold for scrap in 1962, after five years in reserve. (*Royal New Zealand Navy Museum GN 5281*)

HMNZS *Royalist* (1942) Bellona class. Coming alongside the photographic vessel in this 1965 view, the *Royalist* exhibits few changes since joining the RNZN in 1956. Most obvious are the removal of the STAAG twin Bofors ahead of the bridge and the provision of modern life-raft containers. Just prior to transfer she had been modernized at Devonport on similar lines to the *Birmingham*, but with three STAAG Mk2 twin Bofors (plus two singles) and the Type 275 radar on US-pattern Mk63 directors. The MkI main armament turrets were given sighting hoods similar to those on the MkI* mountings on the battleship *Vanguard*. Commissioned into the RNZN in April 1956, she arrived in New Zealand in December, vice the *Bellona*. She saw operational service during the Malayan emergency, and on 25 July 1957 bombarded terrorist positions inland in the Kota Tinggi area of south east Malaya. The *Royalist* was sold for scrap in 1967. (*Maritime Photo Library 1433*)

PNS *Babur* (1942) Bellona class. This photograph dates from after 1963, when the pennant number had been changed from C84 to 84. Very large jacks and ensigns are being flown. The former HMS *Diadem* had been transferred to Pakistan on 5 July 1957, and became a training ship in 1961. Her pre-transfer refit provided a homogeneous AA battery of three twin and six single Bofors, together with updated radar in the form of Types 293 and 968 on the foremast, while the mainmast, slightly modified since transfer, has an air-warning array, probably Type 281B at its head. The *Babur* was renamed *Jahangir* and relegated to harbour training in 1982, then was broken up in 1985. (*Pakistani Navy*)

BAP *Almirante Grau* (1941) Uganda class. Apart from a change of pennant number from C59 to 81, only a few minor changes have been made since the transfer of HMS *Newfoundland*, the most obvious being the plating-in of the torpedo tube opening. Handed over to the Peruvian Navy on 30 December 1959, she retains the Royal Navy sensor outfit, including Types 274, 277Q, 293Q, 960 and 978. There are modern lightweight MRS8 directors for the MkV Bofors, plus the two AA/SU Mk6 with Type 275 radar for the 4 in. At the end of her modernization in 1952 she was identical in most respects to HMS *Nigeria*/INS *Mysore*, including the streamlined bridge. Renamed *Capitan Quinones* and given the new pennant number 83 on 15 May 1973, she became a static training hulk at Callao and was deleted in 1979. (*Peruvian Navy*)

BAP *Coronel Bolognesi* (1942) Uganda class. HMS *Ceylon* was renamed *Coronel Bolognesi* on 9 February 1960, and is seen leaving Portsmouth shortly after transfer, having changed her pennant number from C30 to 82. Her crew are manning the side. A mid-1950s refit had included the provision of a lattice foremast, a modernized sensor outfit similar to that of the *Almirante Grau* and a homogeneous close-range battery of five twin and eight single Bofors. Four lightweight directors have replaced the three obsolete HADT. (*Royal Naval Museum, Portsmouth*)

ORP *Dragon* (1917) Danae class. Part of Force D for the first month of D Day operations, the *Dragon* is seen at anchor with the Polish ensign flying from the mainmast, after shelling German positions on the French coast. Unfortunately, many features on this print, on both the ship and the land background, have been censored and some detail (e.g. Type 273 radar) lost. During a refit by Cammell Laird HMS *Dragon* had been handed over to the Polish Navy on 15 January 1943, without a change of name. After escorting Russian convoys she received a pre-D-Day refit which brought her armament to five 6 in, one twin 4 in, two quad pom-poms and twelve Oerlikons (four twin and four single). Her torpedo tubes were landed. On 8 July 1944 she was torpedoed and, deemed beyond economical repair, was sunk as part of the Gooseberry breakwater of scuttled ships, at the Mulberry Harbour off Arromanches. (*Polish Naval Association*)

ORP *Conrad* (1918) Danae class. This post-war portrait dates from 1946, with the *Conrad* repainted in overall grey. She flies the Polish ensign at her stern. Transferred to Polish control on 4 October 1944 to replace ORP *Dragon*, HMS *Danae* was renamed after the Polish-born writer Joseph Conrad. Her wartime duties included convoy escorts and post-war she took part in Red Cross relief and transport work on Scandinavian routes. She returned to Royal Navy control as the *Danae* on 28 September 1946, then was sold for scrap in 1948. (*Polish Naval Association*)

Mersey Class 2nd Class Protected Cruisers – four ships, first laid down in July 1883. Legend displacement 4,050 tons; length and beam 315 ft x 46 ft; power 4,500 ihp for 17 kts; principal armament: two 8 in and ten 6 in guns, two 18 in torpedo tubes (plus two submerged in *Mersey*); protection: deck 3 in (max).

HMSAS *General Botha* (1885). In this photograph the *General Botha* is leaving dry dock at Simon's Town on 19 July 1933 after refit. The hull remains virtually unaltered, with the five broadside 6 in gun sponsons evident, and the conning tower, bridge and lower masts still intact. The royal coat-of-arms at her prow is in full colour and the elaborate scrollwork is carefully picked out. HMS *Thames* had become a submarine depot ship in 1903 and was sold to South Africa in 1920, becoming the training ship HMSAS *General Botha* at the Cape. In 1942 she reverted to her original name and served as an accommodation ship until 1945. She was scuttled in Simon's Bay in 1947. The first cruisers designed to have no reliance on sail, the Merseys were significant ships, being also the first cruisers with a full-length protective deck. They are thought to have been inspired by the British-built Chilean *Esmeralda*. Although overgunned, the Merseys were good sea boats and the best cruisers to date when new. (*Simon's Town Museum*)

APPENDIX

THE DEVELOPMENT OF FIRE CONTROL AND RADAR

This short section is a brief and non-technical survey of the progression of fire control and target-finding, as applicable to the ships featured in these pages. The aim is to allow the identification of visual features without recourse to repetitive lists of data in successive photograph captions. No attempt is made to explain the detailed workings of the equipment mentioned.

From the introduction of ship-killing guns at sea at the turn of the fifteenth/sixteenth centuries, until a substantial way through the nineteenth century, there was no technology in this area. Hitting a target in the era of smooth-bore muzzle-loaders was dependent on the skilled eye of, at first, a ship's gunner, and later, as rates of fire progressed beyond rounds per day, to that of individual gun captains.

With the longer ranges which rifled guns permitted came first the spotting telescope and later the coincidence rangefinder. Some other navies used the alternative stereoscopic type: both had advantages and disadvantages.

Stronger guns and improved propellants, both of which increased achievable accurate ranges, together with the introduction of multi-turret main armaments, led to the introduction of the gunnery director, a mechanism for getting all guns on to the future position of a target at an accurate bearing and fairly accurate elevation. The director came into widespread use in newer ships during the First World War. However, it relied on separate range-finders, and in post-war designs the Director (which was fitted to less than a handful of pre-Dreadnought cruisers) gave way to the Director Control Tower or DCT for main armament. The post-Washington Treaty Kents were the earliest to be built with a new style of director, the first of these bridge-mounted systems being the Forward Director Tower (FDT) – which were complemented by a less capable Aft Director Tower (ADT). These drum- or box-like structures were unwelcome topweight, especially as an improved 8 in DCT weighed over 11 tons and the prototype armoured 6 in DCT installed in the *Enterprise* weighed some 12.5 tons. Production versions fitted to the Leanders onwards were unarmoured. A special DCT for 5.25 in guns was also produced, and there were variants of most.

An increasing awareness of the threat posed by air attack, coupled with the steadily improving performance of aircraft, led to the introduction of the High-Angle Control System (HACS), the visible portion of which was the High-Angle Director Tower (HADT). This was designed to fulfil the functions of the DCT, together with the added complications of coping with a target moving rapidly in three dimensions, and of the trajectory of AA shells at altitude. The basic system ranged through MksI–V (the latter not in cruisers) and, despite the wartime fitment of radar and other improvements, always lagged behind aircraft performance. Indeed, the only cruiser with adequate high-angle fire control during the Second World War was the *Delhi*, which was fitted with

US-pattern Mk37 directors. A completely new system, owing nothing to earlier marks and designed around Type 275 radar, was known as the HA/LA MkVI HADT, and later as the AA/SU Mk6, and first went to sea before the end of the war, but was just too late to see action. The most numerous version was the MkIV, fitted in twos or threes to all cruisers from the *Glasgow* to the *Swiftsure*. Excepting the AA conversions the older cruisers did not receive a full outfit of modern fire control systems. Indeed, apart from the *Delhi*, the C and D classes got nothing.

From the beginning of 1941 onwards, all marks of DCT, DT and HADT were fitted with radar, as the availability of sets permitted: types 284 and later 274 on DCTs and 285 on DTs and all marks of HADT up to (in cruisers) IV. Radar did not supplant range-finders until after the Second World War.

However, it was not for gunnery but for early warning that radar first appeared, HMS *Sheffield* receiving the first trial installation of Type 79Y in 1938. Each aerial for this, with the transmitting set at the head of the mainmast and the receiving set at the head of the foremast, was basically a pair of horizontal Hs, set above one another. This set gave warning of approaching aircraft only, but a more sophisticated version, which had some capability for detecting surface targets, entered widespread service as Type 279, using a similar aerial. A more capable refinement using pairs of double-Hs emerged as Type 281, which again needed two sets. The development of transceivers enabled a single aerial of either Type 279 or 281 on the mainmast to do the job of two, thereby becoming Type 279B or 281B. Both were in service by the middle of the war, and few cruisers received the post-war replacement Type 960, with an aerial based on Type 281B and always linked to the slab aerial of Interrogation Friend or Foe (IFF) Type X. Many other radars prior to Type 960 also had associated IFF aerials.

Although most aerials were exposed to the elements, those of the first dedicated surface warning sets, Types 271–73, were housed in protective 'lanterns'. These were at first teak frameworks with perspex panels, and were later moulded in one piece. Type 273 was the largest, commonest and most capable, while Type 272 was a smaller lightweight version which was placed on the foremast starfish of classes such as the Didos and Fijis. The next surface warning set, Type 277, had a circular parabolic mesh aerial. This developed into Types 277Q and 278 post-war, using a similar but larger aerial which was a dished circle with cropped sides. Later combined HA/LA warning radars such as Types 293, 293Q and 992, which were placed at the vacant head of the foremast in ships that received Types 279B, 281B or 960, used 'cheese' aerials of various sizes, although the earliest combined radars (Types 286 and 291) employed aerials which traced their ancestry to Types 279 or 281. Some radars, such as the foremast-mounted Type 978, also aided navigation.

Gunnery radar for main armament (5.25 in upwards) was at first confined to Type 284 with its large (21 ft) aerial (which was split into more than one section in some ships) mounted on the forward DCT. This was later replaced in many ships by the 14 ft double cheese aerial of Type 274. Because of shortages, a few ships had to make do with yagi aerials, normally associated with AA directors, for the DCT's Type 284 set.

Close-range armament had its own systems. The quad 0.5 in machine-gun mountings and single automatic guns of heavier calibres were aimed through open sights, whereas multiple pom-poms had directors which were fitted with Type 282 radar after mid-1941. Main armament guns could also be used for AA barrage fire, using directors with Type 283, both radars using two of the six yagi elements and reflectors from Type 285. The twin circular reflectors of Type 275 on HADT MkVI had covers and looked like huge kettle drums.

Post-war, some cruisers landed their HADTs to reduce topweight and instead employed radar Type 262, with its small dish aerial, to direct high-angle fire. These dishes were mounted either on 4 in gun shields or in small modern MRS8 directors. The conventional cruisers had nothing better than modified wartime Type 274 for main armament to the end. However, the three redesigned Tiger class ships received the most modern radars, with Type 903 on new MRS3 directors, Type 960 for air warning, and Types 992 and 277Q fore and aft for surface/air warning and target indication. When the *Blake* and *Tiger* were converted to carry helicopters they received Types 965, with its 1.25 ton 'bedstead' aerial, 26 ft wide and some 9 ft high, and 278. The 'bedstead' had IFF Type 10 (Type X redesignated) at the top edge.

In the Royal Navy radar was known as Radio Direction Finding (RDF) until 1943.

Some Aerial Systems on British Cruisers.

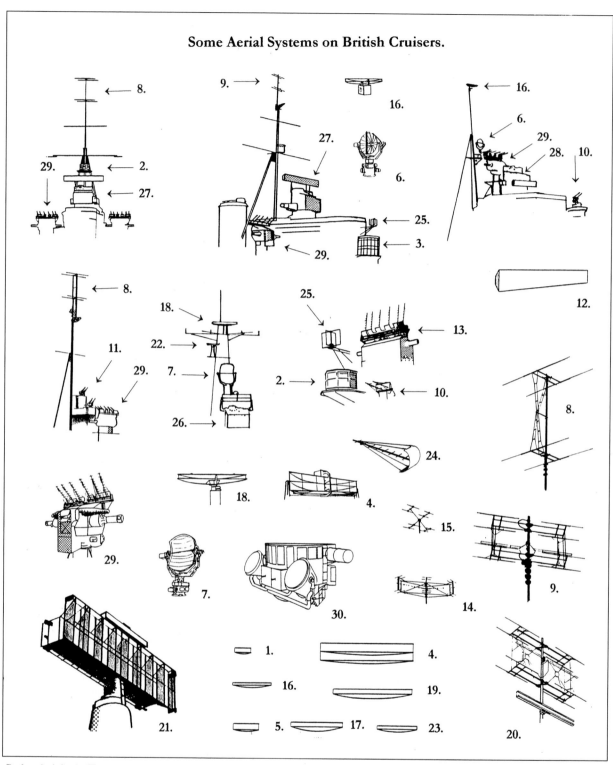

Radar Aerials: 1. Type 268; 2 T272; 3. T273; 4. T274; 5. T276; 6. T277; 7. T277Q; 8. T279 or 279B*; 9. T281 or 281B*; 10. T282; 11. T283; 13. T284 with yagi aerials on 6 in DCT; 14. T286; 15. T291; 16. T293; 17. T293M; 18. T293Q; 19. T293Q or 992; 20. T960 + IFF MkX; 21. T965 + IFF Mk10; 22. T978; 23. T974 or 978; 24. single yagi (two on T282 and 283, six on T284 and 285); *Misc*: 25. MF/DF; 26. 6 in DCT with T274; 27. 6 in DCT with T284; 28. 5.25 in DCT with T284; 29. HADT MkIV with T285; 30. HADT MkVI (later AA/SU Mk6) with T275.

*B versions are single-mast systems.

GLOSSARY

AA:	Anti-Aircraft
ADT:	Aft Director Tower (see FDT)
AMC:	Armed Merchant Cruiser (an offensively armed liner or merchant ship serving in wartime as an auxiliary cruiser)
ASDIC:	(Allied Submarine Detection Investigation Committee) an echolocation device for detecting submarines
av:	average
BAP:	Buque Armada Peruano (Peruvian Navy warship)
Bofors:	Swedish 40 mm 2 pdr automatic light anti-aircraft gun on single, twin or quadruple mountings
camouflage:	a paint scheme designed to conceal the presence or true size of a ship
carley floats:	buoyant life-saving rafts
Cdre:	Commodore – a naval rank between Captain and Rear-Admiral
CinC:	Commander-in-Chief
cm:	centimetre
CS:	Cruiser Squadron: also Chinese Nationalist Navy warship
dazzle:	a paint scheme designed to make the assessment of a ship's speed and/or bearing more difficult, or to confuse range-taking
DCT:	Director Control Tower
DF:	Direction-Finder/Finding (of radio signals)
displacement:	The weight of water displaced by a ship equals its weight, including its contents at that moment. The official tonnage of a warship includes various consumables, such as a percentage of fuel. In early years the formula used produced legend displacement. International agreement reached within the 1922 Washington Naval Treaty produced standard displacement. Both figures were well below the maximum laden weight of a ship
DP:	Dual-Purpose
embrasure:	a recessed gunport cut to allow axial fire
FDT:	Forward Director Tower (transitional main armament control tower on 8 in cruisers, prior to fitting of a full DCT)
ft:	foot/feet
grt:	gross registered tons (weight measurement of merchant ships, based on enclosed volume)
HA:	High-Angle
HADT:	High-Angle Director Tower; the visible part of a High-Angle Control System (HACS)
HF/DF:	High-Frequency Direction-Finder
HIJMS:	His Imperial Japanese Majesty's Ship
HMS:	Her/His Majesty's Ship
HMAS:	His Majesty's Australian Ship
HMCS:	Her/His Majesty's Canadian Ship
HMIS:	His Majesty's Indian Ship
HMNZS:	Her/His Majesty's New Zealand Ship
HMSAS:	His Majesty's South African Ship
HT:	High Tensile
IFF:	Identification Friend or Foe
ihp:	indicated horsepower – the power output of steam reciprocating engines
in:	inch/inches

INS:	Indian Navy Ship	**RFA:**	Royal Fleet Auxiliary
kt:	knot/knots	**RMS:**	Royal Mail Steamer
LA:	Low-Angle	**RN:**	Reale Nave (Royal Italian Navy warship); to avoid confusion, RN has not been used as an abbreviation for Royal Navy in these pages
LCS:	Light Cruiser Squadron		
MAS:	Motoscafo Silurante (motor torpedo boat)		
MF/DF:	Medium-Frequency Direction-Finder		
mm:	millimetre	**RNZN:**	Royal New Zealand Navy
MFV:	Motor Fishing Vessel (used as a fleet tender)	**sheathed:**	Before effective anti-fouling paints were introduced, steel ships built primarily for tropical service were clad (sheathed) underwater with a layer of wood-backed copper to deter marine growth which would otherwise produce drag and thus reduce range and speed
MRS:	Medium-Range System		
MV:	Merchant Vessel		
Oerlikon:	Swiss 20 mm automatic light anti-aircraft gun on single or twin mountings		
ORP:	Okręt Rzeczypospolitej Polskiej (Polish Navy warship)	**shp:**	shaft horsepower – the power output of steam turbine engines
pdr:	pounder (as in the weight of a shell fired from an automatic or other light gun)	**SMS:**	Seiner Majestät Schiff (Imperial German Navy warship)
PNS:	Pakistan Navy Ship	**STAAG:**	Stabilized Tachymetric Anti-Aircraft Gun
pom-pom:	Vickers 40 mm 2 pdr automatic light anti-aircraft gun on single, quadruple or octuple mountings	**transom:**	a square-cut stern, which offered greater speed and efficiency
QF:	Quick-Firing – 'fixed' ammunition with the shell attached to the cartridge case	**UP:**	Unrotated Projectile
		USN:	United States Navy
quad:	quadruple, i.e. four guns on one mounting	**USS:**	United States Ship
		VAd:	Vice-Admiral
RAd:	Rear-Admiral	**VC:**	Victoria Cross
RAN:	Royal Australian Navy	**wooded:**	aim or view obscured by ship's structure
RCN:	Royal Canadian Navy	**W/T:**	Wireless Telegraphy
RD:	Rangefinder-Director	**2i/c:**	second-in-command

BIBLIOGRAPHY

Archibald, E.H.H., *The Fighting Ship of the Royal Navy AD 897–1984*, New York, 1987

Brown, D.K., *Warrior to Dreadnougt*, London, 1997

Brown, D.K., *The Grand Fleet*, London, 1999

Brown, J.D. (ed), *The British Pacific and East Indies Fleets – 50th Anniversary*, Liverpool, 1995

Burt, R.A., *British Cruisers of World War One*, Poole, 1987

Corbett, Sir J. & Newbolt Sir H., *Official History of the* [First World] *War: Naval Operations* (5 vols), London, 1920–31

Fraccaroli, A., *Italian Warships of World War Two*, Shepperton, 1968

Friedman, N., *Naval Radar*, Greenwich, 1981

Gardiner, R. (ed), *Conway's All the World's Fighting Ships* (four volumes), London, 1979–85

Hodges, P., *Royal Navy Warship Camouflage*, New Malden, 1973

Howse, D., *Radar at Sea: the Royal Navy in World War Two*, London, 1993

Jentschura, H., Jung, J., & Mickel, P., transl. Brown, J.D., & Preston A., *Warships of the Imperial Japanese Navy, 1869–1945*, London, 1966

Lenton, H.T., *German Surface Vessels* (2 vols), London, 1966

Morris, D., *Cruisers of the Royal and Commonwealth Navies*, Liskeard, 1987

Raven, A., 'The Development of Naval Camouflage 1914–1945,' in *Plastic Ship Modeller*, various edns, Arvada, 1996/97

Raven, A., & Roberts, J., *British Cruisers of World War Two*, London, 1980

Rohwer, J., & Hummelchen, G., *Chronology of the War at Sea 1939–1945* (2nd edn), London, 1992

Roskill, S.W., *Official History of the Second World War: The War at Sea* (3 vols), London, 1954–61

Sainsbury, A.B., (ed.) *The Royal Navy Day by Day*, Shepperton, 1992

Whitley, M.J., *Cruisers of World War Two*, London, 1995

INDEX OF PHOTOGRAPHS